# WANDER

## A MEMOIR OF LETTING GO
## AND WALKING 2,000 MILES
## TO A MEANINGFUL LIFE.

## RYAN BENZ

*To my children:*

*Be bold.*

*Take risks.*

*Follow your heart and create your own path.*

# AUTHOR'S NOTE

To write this book, I relied on my personal journals, researched facts whenever possible, consulted with several of the people who appear in the book, and drew upon my own memory. There are parts that I have simplified for clarity. What can I say, a lot happened. I have changed the names of some individuals for the purpose of anonymity when I felt it was needed, and in rare cases, omitted people and events only when that omission had no significant impact on the overall story. Read this as you would a long story while sitting around a campfire with friends.

# THE APPALACHIAN TRAIL

## GEORGIA TO MAINE

# CONTENTS

# INTRODUCTION

## PERMISSION TO WANDER

One thing I have come to know is that a new path is always possible; we just need to choose it for ourselves.

Imagine waking up one day and realizing everything you chose for your life was making you feel the opposite of how you hoped it would. That's where I was, and I had reached a breaking point. Panic attacks came first, then ultimately thoughts of ending everything. I always thought I was okay, until the day I wasn't.

It took everything in me during those most difficult months just to wake up every day and keep going. Until one of those days, I realized that the only thing that needed to end was the version of me that believed I was trapped with no way out. Once I gave myself permission to choose the path ahead, the crippling fear and anxiety fell away. That's what I share with you in this book: how I did it, why I did it, and all the beauty revealed along the way.

A new path might be internal—a shift in mindset, a new way to see old things, yourself, or the world. It might be exter-nal, such as a change in vocation, where you live, or something as simple as a habit. Very often, the changes we make are both inside and out, one influencing the other, hand in hand.

That's how it was for me. I was blindly heading down one path, unaware, sleepwalking, stepping but not feeling the ground, looking but not really seeing. I'm convinced now, in this present day, that I have lived two completely different lives: one before the trail, separated by over five million steps from the one I live now. But it wasn't truly the miles that divide these two paths.

For a new path to be possible for me, I had to let go of what was holding me to the old one. I had to take a chance on my dreams, the ones that came from my own heart. I had to give myself permission to wander.

This is not a trail guide or a "how-to" for hiking the Appalachian Trail. It is not another thru-hike to inspire you into the two-thousand-plus miles from Springer Mountain in Georgia to Mount Katahdin in Maine. That is where this story unfolds but not what it is about. There are plenty of guides available on the shelves, and if you are planning to take on the AT, you should read them.

This is a book about hope—the hope I had that change is possible in a world so entrenched in what is practical. It is a look at the internal transformation that occurs when you allow yourself to hope and then wander toward that hope. For me, that meant walking along a path in the woods.

I didn't know I needed this story until I had lived it. And once I had, I knew I needed to write it. In many ways, it is the story I wished someone would have told me when I was young, one of options and possibilities. In that way, I hope it is also not just a story for me but for anyone feeling lost, stressed, or burned out, anyone ignoring the needs they feel buried deep down in their gut.

I share many lessons learned along that path and perhaps just as many unlearned, and I hope you'll forgive me for that. They are as intrinsic to this journey as the decision to begin it and as much a part of my current heart-led life as air or water. I hope a few of them will resonate with you like they did with me. But there is no lesson in these pages that I learned or share as important as the title itself—*Wander*.

After living a life of rigidity in hopes of carving out my small corner of the American Dream, I found myself unhappy, unsatisfied, and unfulfilled with that dream. I didn't know what that meant. Looking around my sphere in the corporate world, no one seemed any happier. I knew I wanted something different, something that felt right, that felt true to who I was, but there were no examples to be found where I was, no model to which I could aspire.

There were, of course, examples, but I didn't know where to look to find them. They weren't around me. And that was the key—I needed to look somewhere else. I needed to wander. It didn't really matter where. Because it wasn't really the journey or the destination I was lacking; those were just byproducts. What I needed was simply to make the choice for myself. And that's what I did. I gave myself permission to wander, to rethink my internal and external. I took a long walk through the woods and found myself on the other side. I hope you will too.

# 1

## A NEW IDENTITY

My old life lay behind; a better one ahead. The day was bright and clear. I basked in the warm euphoria of the perfect adventure in front of me. Beckoning me forward was a worn stone archway, like a portal to the new me. A freshly painted brown wooden sign stood to its left on two weathered posts. White letters read:

APPALACHIAN TRAIL APPROACH
SPRINGER MTN., GA. 8.5 MILES
MT. KATAHDIN, MAINE 2,108.5 MILES

I read the words and was unphased. It could have said 200,000 miles, and I would have felt the same. I was invincible.

The sign was, in fact, wrong; the trail from Springer Mountain to Mount Katahdin was actually 2,189.8 miles long that year, a fact I knew from countless hours of research. It didn't matter. I forgave its error. I wanted to be weathered like the sign and archway, marked by all I was about to endure, unconcerned about fact-checking myself. In some ways, I already was. The past ten years had beaten me down, mostly of my own doing. I wanted a different sort of weathering now, the kind you catch in the mirror, and it makes you smile and wince with memory, the kind you only gain from finding out what you're made of. Standing in that archway, I knew I was exactly where I needed to be, doing what I wanted to do. But if the Appalachian Trail had a voice in that moment, I think it might have said, "Ryan, how little you know."

It did have a voice, of sorts…many voices, each belonging to people like me hoping for their own version of transformation on a long, wooded walk.

One voice was Tommy's. A Montreal native, his first language was French, and his English came in short bursts with lots of hand gestures, pointing to a gnarled tree or a granite boulder wading in a clear stream. Tommy and I got to know each other that morning, as much as his vocabulary would permit, on the shuttle from the Hiker Hostel. Our conversation was a stark contrast to the office breakroom chatter I'd grown so numbly accustomed to, before I ditched the watercooler for good.

"And we step," said Tommy, as we both stood staring at the stone archway with the wooden sign beside it.

"Now or never," I said, and like skydivers stepping out into the vast openness beyond a perfectly good airplane, we were out on our own, hiking that wooded vastness with ancient mountains and dark vales known as the Appalachian Trail. Well, not quite. We still had to complete a moderate day-one climb from Amicalola Falls to Springer Mountain, the official southern terminus of the trail.

I felt prepared. Like most who set out to thru-hike a long-distance trail, I had spent the previous many months planning. I picked up books by past thru-hikers, studied guides filled with descriptions of every town, resting place, and resupply stop, and learned about things called Trail Angels, Trail Magic, and various other lingo. I loaded all the gear I needed into a spreadsheet, including their listed weight down to the ounce. Recent life events had taught me to weigh carefully what I carried with me with an emphasis on less, so shaving my pack down to essentials was more than practical hiking strategy—it was instinctive for me, the way a person might shy away from strange dogs after being bitten.

I planned how I would eat on the trail healthily, with a balance of clean proteins, carbs, and fiber, and I considered all those micronutrients as well. I even had a mental and emotional wellness strategy—I would celebrate the little moments, as many as I could find, and would carry logbooks to write in every day: who I met, what was interesting, and most importantly, one thing that made me grateful—a simple question, "What made me happy today?".

I had spent the last several months trying to forge a better relationship with myself, my goals, my expectations, what I valued, and where I spent my time and energy. I hoped to use the trail as a reconditioning tool, to stop looking so far ahead and find true pleasure in the present moment. I had steeped myself in knowledge of the great masters, sayings like "To travel well is better than to arrive," and, "The journey is the reward." I was shedding my life of destinations with only a bare tolerance for the journeys between them.

I also knew the hike couldn't just be about me. I had come to believe life was best lived in service to others. In my career, I'd spent some of my business development hours volunteering for a program aimed at benefiting people suffering from cystic fibrosis, an inherited life-threatening disease that impacts the lungs and affects one's ability to breathe over time. The giant 17oz flag with the moniker I'd created "Breathtaking Journey" stitched across the fabric became the only "non-essential" essential in my bag.

My hopes for the trail buoying me, I believed I was prepared for whatever the nearly 2,200 miles and 464,464 feet of elevation gain and loss through fourteen states could throw at me. A trail that takes, on average, half a year to complete and sends 75% of attempters back home before the end. I had always taken care of my body, and thirty-five pounds of pack seemed like a manageable burden.

Then there was Tommy beside me, much taller and stockier of build. His steps were loud and heavy with big, rugged leather hiking boots strapped to his trunks and a pack jammed with enough food for three weeks without resupply. Even with all that weight, he hiked with the speed of a Clydesdale horse pulling an entire freight behind him. Even the aviator sunglasses covering his face contributed to his appearance of no-nonsense badassery. Then he would speak, and I remembered...he was more a life-sized French-Canadian teddy bear. Nonetheless, the man appeared formidable striding up the 604 steps and 729 vertical feet of Amicalola Falls that morning. Many thru-hikers skip this part and take the road directly to Springer Mountain. They miss the waterfall and save the energy. Preparing for that morning, I couldn't blame them, but since my plan was to hike all 2,189.8 miles, I felt good about absorbing the additional 8.8. After the seven cascades of Amicalola Falls, I began doubting both my abilities and decision-making.

Watching Tommy fly up the falls seemingly without effort didn't make things any easier. I was tempted to feel a little down about myself, gulping in frantic breaths behind him under the weight of my relatively light pack. And there I was, day one—day zero, really—and I was already falling victim to the same flawed mindset that had trapped me in my previous life. Tommy was the "Jones," and I was failing to "keep up." But the trail guides had prepared me. Repeated in nearly all of the many trail preparation guides I'd read was the acronym HYOH—Hike Your Own Hike. Why hadn't I heard that in any of the lectures on college campus?

I shut my eyes hard against the image of my pack-mule hiking companion ahead of me for a few steps… *You have your own pack, Ryan. And your own legs. Hike your own hike.*

"HYOH!" I shouted, and immediately felt embarrassed at my own corniness. But it was the kind of embarrassment that didn't make you feel small, the kind you could immediately laugh at. Tommy helped with that.

"HYOH!" he echoed back.

I heard myself laughing, and realization hit me—if I had enough air in my lungs to laugh, I had enough to hike.

We stopped at the top of the falls and looked down and caught our breaths, mine at least, before moving on. I busied my mind with facts I knew about the scene before me—the height in feet, the number of cascades and stair steps to the top, the fact that these were the third tallest falls east of the Mississippi River. I had a fleeting feeling of having surmounted something great, then was quickly shocked back into reality, that I hadn't even reached the actual Appalachian Trail yet.

The rest of the approach was a rollercoaster, filled with the embodiment of another bit of trail lingo—PUDs, pointless ups and downs. Arriving at the base of these many hills, you are filled with excitement, wondering what the view at the top will be like. Reaching the crest, any glimpse of the world around it blocked thick with trees and underbrush, you wonder why the original blazers didn't just go around.

After finishing the additional 8.8 miles of hiking, Tommy and I officially reached the top of Springer Mountain and the southern terminus of the Appalachian Trail. I snapped a photo with a sign which read, "A footpath for those who seek fellowship with the wilderness."

That was a noble goal, I thought as we continued forward onto the official beginning of the trail. Fellowship with the wilderness was certainly part of what I came here for. *Part...* I let the word settle in my head. What was the rest? What had I actually left an entire life behind for? I couldn't put those words together, not here in these first steps on the trail. *I've come here to figure out what I came here for,* I settled on and kept stepping.

By the end of day one, I had hiked only 2.8 miles of the actual AT and fought the urge to wonder again whether I should have skipped the approach trail. The straps of my pack had left my waist and shoulders chafed and agitated to the point of bleeding, and my legs were broken down in a way I had never felt inside a gym or on the many short trails I frequented as a child. I shook on swollen, throbbing knees and ankles as I set up my shelter that first night. I felt like I had stepped into the ring with a professional boxer paid by the punch.

Despite the pain, the smile I wore was undiminishable. There was nothing like being out in the open wilderness of the trail. My lungs felt like they had doubled in size. My pack had been surprisingly and agonizingly heavy, but in every other way, I felt light. That was a feeling unknown to me in the pharmaceutical marketing industry. There, someone waited around every fluorescent corner to tell me what I should be doing and how I should be doing it, an experience I called being "should on". It wasn't until I left that career that I realized just how much the "should on" experience extended beyond the corporate walls, how there's this template laid out for us that we *should* be following, one that *should* lead to a happy and successful life. But what happens when we follow that template only to realize everything we were told we *should* want isn't actually what we *do* want?

By contrast, on the trail, in the woods, "should" didn't need an outside interpreter, an administrator of my movements. "Should" was always obvious, simply by opening my eyes and ears. There was the trail ahead of me, the sound of the creek beside me. I was as free as free got, and I drank it in with every aching cell.

At camp near Stover Creek Shelter, everything was new, like visiting a place I had dreamed of going. I pulled each item out of my pack inside my tent, and though I could tell you the weight in ounces of each, it was like seeing them for the first time. This was their true environment, and I hoped it was mine. The plan for the evening was to cook dry lentils, quinoa, and pumpkin seeds, the perfect meal to heal my screaming body, then get as much sleep as a first night on the trail would allow. Tomorrow would be another magical day of adventure.

I found a safe, flat place in the dirt and settled my small propane canister, positioned my cook pot over it, and began boiling my food. I'd never cooked these particular dried goods before, but I had cooked instant rice. This couldn't be much different. I grabbed a journal and used the few available minutes to scratch down the events of my first day. After about five minutes, I peeked over the rim of my pot at a slurry of nearly still water, no sign whatsoever of the fire blazing beneath it. I turned the flame slightly up. It was ten minutes before bubbles began blooping up from the base of the pot… and another few minutes before they had turned into a timid boil. I gave the situation another five minutes and spooned out a few seeds to test. They were like pieces of iron. I glanced down at the propane canister and back at the hard bits in my spoon. Another five minutes, and they would be ready, I told myself. Just another five minutes, and even if they are a little hard, it wouldn't be a problem. I wasn't out here for the luxury of it, after all. I waited seven minutes more for good measure. With all the satisfaction of having cooked my first meal on the trail, I shoveled a large helping into my mouth and bit down on what may as well have been a pile of gravel.

I could afford no more fuel on this meal. I chewed until the pieces were fractured enough to swallow, and then I muscled down several more mouthfuls of barely cooked lentils, quinoa, and pumpkin seeds until my jaw was sore and began to click. Frustrated and stomach still growling, I set up my bed and closed my eyes. One day down, one intention—the one to eat healthy on the trail—broken. I was okay, I told myself. I had been through worse in life and would go through worse still on this trail. Experiences like these required adjustments, and I was ready to make them. This was just part of the weathering process.

\*\*\*

"Every day, it will get easier."

That's what a thru-hiker told me the next morning as I made my way from camp. I was on a course for Woody Gap that day, and he was finishing up the southern half of the trail. He had hiked everything north of Harpers Ferry, West Virginia, the previous year.

"Not the trail," he clarified, chuckling. "Your body will adjust."

I appreciated the encouragement, enough that I didn't tell him what I wanted to say, that I already knew yesterday's nearly twelve miles, difficult as they were, would be considerably easier than today's 17.8. The pain in my legs and from my straps was already present before I took my first step. And the forecast of rain and hail was heavy on my mind. Tommy and I ran into each other several times that day. I would catch up to him resting, and we would go on together for a few miles. Then I would need a snack, and he would go on ahead. Anytime he was there with me, I kept my usual smile and calm demeanor plastered on my face, but inside, I was tamping down a quickly-growing fear that I had overestimated my ability to do this.

Mixed in with the pain were moments of awe, though. The trail through that stretch of Georgia is a non-stop series of climbs and descents through forest characterized by pines and old oaks, and thick underbrush. Views are dominated by the green tunnel with only rare glimpses beyond. But then suddenly, the trail would wind outward onto the edge of a bluff or crest over a rise and reward you with a spectacular vista stretching many miles. The lush, deep greens of the trail disappear into a soft blue horizon, and you feel you could cup the whole stretch of landscape in your hands. These moments, combined with my interminable stubbornness, kept me focused on the trail.

The next day was not so kind. We had hoped to make it up and over Blood Mountain before the rain hit, but the system shifted south early. Angry-looking clouds boiled over us as Tommy and two new thru-hikers I'd met, Scuba Steve and Eric, frantically stuffed our campsite back into our packs that morning at Woody Gap. The forecasted hail never became a reality, but the rain was cold out of the north, and it wasn't long before I had to clench my teeth to quiet their chattering. Blood Mountain, an already daunting anticipation of our first truly difficult ascent and descent, was transformed by the weather into a treacherous one. Every painful, shivering step was slowed by the threat of slipping over the many steep and sometimes sheer edges. Views from the trail, including from the summit, were fully covered in gray, cold, wet air. "I warned you," the trail might have said then.

Just past the Blood Mountain Shelter, as we began our descent, I decided to quickly switch from my soaked shirt into a dry one. I had thrown my rain jacket on when the shivering set in during the ascent, but warmth never came. I found a flat spot amid the downslope, stripped off my jacket, and began the process of peeling my soaked shirt off, like trying to remove casing from a sausage. After a couple of hard tugs, my thumb broke through the fabric, and I was suddenly holding the disembodied collar of my shirt.

It was easier to tear the rest of the shirt off, relegating it from clothing to scraps of cloth that might come in handy. It was less easy to keep the inside of my rain jacket dry while doing all of this. I must have looked like a madman from a distance, half-naked, fumbling around in the cold rain on the side of a mountain. Later, I managed to laugh at myself for attempting this in the deluge, no more than a mile after passing the perfectly dry Blood Mountain Shelter.

I managed to get a mostly-dry replacement shirt on and covered with my rain jacket. Relief waited for us at the base of Blood Mountain—a well-known outfitter called Mountain Crossings directly on the trail. Hiking boots hung from the lower branches of a large tree outside, and from the exposed rafters of the lodge-style store, evidence of the many footwear changes the trail forces, both from mileage and poor fit. My own feet were blistered from the rain and miles. I'd read many horror stories about whole pads of calluses becoming softened and sloughing off, leaving raw exposed flesh. There was little I could do; no matter how waterproof my trail runners were, the non-stop rain eventually found its way in. But I had a greater concern than even this—the pinky toe on my right foot was in trouble. I'd felt a little pressure inside the shoe starting out. When I removed my socks at the end of day one, the small toe was red, while its brothers were their normal shade of pink. The next day, it began hurting in earnest, and had not stopped since. But the shoes were brand new with hundreds of miles of tread left. Rather than giving in to worry, I chalked the discomfort up to early hike adjustments my body needed to make.

While browsing for resupply items, I overheard Tommy chatting about his goals with a staff member.

"Three months," he said.

It was the first I'd heard him mention wanting to complete the trail that quickly.

"Three months?" said the staff member.

"Whole complete," answered Tommy in his French-Canadian accent.

"Well… Might I suggest a shakedown?"

One of the most helpful services offered by Mountain Crossings and many other outfitters along the trail is a "shakedown" by an experienced thru-hiker. Despite careful decisions before setting out, I had already shaken down a few items from my own pack and didn't feel a need to consult the experts. Tommy, on the other hand, was still lugging about twenty pounds more than me.

"What are you… You don't need *half* of this food," said the expert.

"Throw away?" I could hear the panic in Tommy's voice at the prospect of trashing valuable calories.

"In the garbage? No, just mail it to yourself."

"But I'm here. Why mail?"

"Not here. Up the trail."

It took some coaxing, and a lot of arduous translating, but in the end, Tommy's pack was reduced to nearly the same weight as mine, and a box full of food was bound for a location further up-trail to be retrieved later. He left Mountain Crossings with even more bounce in his steps; I stepped gingerly out with my same trail runners and a resupplied pack.

With the rain driving hikers indoors, we were fortunate to find space at Blood Mountain Cabins that night, less than half a mile from Mountain Crossings. We splurged on pizza and wings, my first "real" meal on the trail. All previous calories had been whatever I could stomach from my dry grain and seed stores, and a few energy bars.

An uplifted mood was the immediate result of a full belly. I wrote in my journal that evening that I was grateful for powering through the first day of rain and tackling Blood Mountain. I imagined the surplus of calories and a good night of sleep in the cabin giving my muscles and feet a chance to recover. That's all my pinky toe really needed. The next day would finally be the beginning of the promised "Every day, it will get easier".

Tommy wouldn't be there to see it, though. True to his expressed pace goals, he was gone before Scuba Steve, Eric, and I woke. I felt a twinge of disappointment. I had only known him a few days, but when the whole current experience of your life could be boiled down to a few days, any constants felt something like home, and he was that. We had taken our first steps on the Appalachian Trail together, after all. But there were many more miles to hike and, no doubt, people to meet. Had he been there, he wouldn't have witnessed the reality through my optimism, anyway.

That next day proved no easier than the previous. Though the rains had subsided into intermittent spitting, the winds arrived just in time to replace them. Every gust wicked away what little warmth I felt, cold enough to keep me shivering, but not enough to numb the deep bruising on my shoulders and hips, not to mention my right pinky toe, now throbbing with every cold step as it rubbed against my constricting shoes. Eric and I began the day together and met up with another hiker called Red Bull. Like Scuba Steve—who had slept in a little later that morning—Red Bull was his trail name. Every thru-hiker eventually earned a trail name, traditionally given by another hiker. Our new companion was a lumberjack-looking character with bright red hair and stubble to match. We needed no other explanation for how he became Red Bull.

Red Bull, Eric, and I found ourselves hiking the same pace and stayed together all 18.8 miles of that fourth day. The weather remained gray, and visibility remained limited, but walking with others helped take my mind off the pain, just a bit, and enough that I found myself appreciating simply walking on a dirt path surrounded by greenery amid fog.

By midday, walking no longer felt simple. Large rocks and crevices filled with mud, and hazy pools from the rains choked the path, and I did my best to hide the constant winces. I wondered how the others seemed so unaffected, as though they felt no pain, and the cold wet brought them comfort. They seemed strong, blessed with the legs of mountain goats. I felt slow and weak, tenuously picking my way over the boulders. When my shoes finally landed on a flatter stretch of ground, I stopped and plopped down on one of the larger rocks.

"Scrambler," said Red Bull, as he settled beside me.

"Scrambler?" I said.

"Your Trail Name."

I pictured myself struggling through the previous patch of trail. The name sounded like someone scrambling to barely make it, and I wasn't sure I liked the idea of that being the identity of my trail experience. "Scrambler... Hmm—" I started.

"Yeah!" Red Bull interjected. "I couldn't believe how steady you were over those boulders, like Aladdin floating on his magic carpet. You were really scrambling, man! I was jealous!"

I couldn't believe what Red Bull had just described. Jealous? I had felt anything but steady working my way over those boulders. But from his perspective, I was just that. It made me cringe at just how little credit we give ourselves sometimes. *Scrambler...* The word suddenly meant something completely different, a trail name I could be proud of.

"Scrambler, I'll take it!" I said.

The rest of that day, I had a different outlook. If I looked competent with all the pain and discomfort I was in, how much had they been dealing with? Comparison... That's what the rat race had been about. I didn't want to bring habits I'd picked up onto the trail with me. I opened up for the first time and mentioned my toe's soreness that night, and Red Bull told me about how he too had concerns about his feet and would be taping his toes. Eric chimed in that his pack was feeling uncomfortable, and we all agreed that the pack-chafing of our shoulders and waists was the bane of our trail existence. Suddenly, I was no longer the only one struggling.

We made it 18.8 miles to Blue Mountain Shelter that day, and even though my pack was still soaked, and I was cold and wet and sore, I wore a real smile on my face that night. I was no longer Ryan Benz, who had come to hike the Appalachian Trail alone, or Ryan Benz, who had overestimated himself. I was Scrambler, thru-hiker, one of many.

# 2

## PRESENCE OF OTHERS

The next morning, I think I heard ice shatter inside my joints as I slowly reanimated to life. It took me several minutes to stand, and my fingers burned with cold while I pushed items back inside my pack. The rains had left us, but the wind had howled all night, and despite the near-constant battering of our campsite, I was just as wet and cold that morning as I had been the day before. I winced through every cinch and clasp putting on my pack and wondered with unspoken but fully articulated thoughts whether I could make it through this.

A slow, agonizing descent down from the shelter brought us along a ridge and deposited us at a trailhead parking lot in Unicoi Gap by the Hiwassee River. I slowed as we approached the parking lot, bargaining with myself every step. *Why am I even out here? What did I really hope to gain?* I began poking holes in the idea that had so recently felt like the only thing in the world I was sure of, that I was here to figure it out. Then came the emotional counterattack—shame… ashamed of my weakness, worse than the weakness itself, a familiar fear welled up, one I had felt so viscerally when my wife of five years and I had divorced. It had taken me an entire month to tell my family the truth. Here I was again with the fear that I was a quitter, a failure, that I couldn't do this without help. Then, I was too proud to ask for it, too afraid to be vulnerable. Now, was I the same? What help could anyone find out here, anyway?

We stumbled silently into the trailhead parking lot. Years of weather had turned the asphalt into gravel, sand, and mud. The crunch of pebbles beneath my feet was the only backdrop of noise that broke through my thoughts, though faint and far off. My mind was somewhere else and had been the whole of that morning. I was at a crossroads.

I wondered whether my hiking mates felt anything like I did. As I wrestled with the thoughts of inadequacy and shame, worse ones crept into my thinking—how long would it take me to hitchhike into the nearest town? Could I rent a car one-way back to New Jersey?

The sound of gravel beneath slow-moving tires brought me back to the parking lot, and I watched a van pulling in. It was a welcome distraction from the dread that had begun to fill up my anxious mind. The vehicle stopped, and within seconds, the doors were flung open and out poured a series of people carrying equipment and bags. Tables were unfolded and bags were unpacked. Within a few minutes, breakfast was being cooked in a small, dilapidated parking lot in the middle of nowhere.

My first experience with trail angels happened on the morning of my fifth day on the Appalachian Trail, and it could not have come at a better time. There was fresh hot coffee, sausage-and-egg sandwiches, and water for resupply. Lawn chairs were unfolded to give us a moment of comfort off our feet. Each volunteer approached me, asking how my hike had gone so far and offering encouragement along with information about the next stretch of miles.

When my stomach was full, I stood with effort and walked toward my bag. I looked down at it for a moment, daunted at how heavy I knew it was. Before I reached down to start the process of hoisting it up, one of the trail angels approached, an older man of about sixty or so years, and stepped in front of me to grab my pack before I could. He picked up my 35-pound pack, slowly walked around behind me, and placed it over my shoulders. I felt a strong urge to tell him that he didn't need to help me, that I could do it myself. This was a man more than twice my age, and I was the one hiking the trail, after all. But I didn't. I was silent while he slowly handed me my trekking poles, like family caring for a soldier returned from war.

For the first time on the trail, I felt some level of validation for just how much I was struggling. Through this man, it's as if I was being told it was ok to struggle, and it was ok to be *seen* struggling. After all, the AT is difficult, so difficult that trail angels exist, and their only purpose is to help you. Because you need it. I needed it.

"There," said the old man, brushing a bit of dirt off my pack and smiling like a father would to a son. "You're all ready now."

"Thank you," I said. I was.

The balance of that day felt much like the morning had, painful steps stacked together, adding up to another stretch of miles covered. Cold wind still gnawed at our faces and fingers, and wet clothes still made us shiver. It was brutally miserable by all accounts. I woke the next day feeling a little more recovered than previous mornings and let my eyes stay closed longer than usual. A rare early sun was slowly warming my tent, and I hoped the same for my clothes. I knew before moving that I was still sorer than I'd ever been before starting the AT, a fact that remained constant each new day, but something had changed—the fear was gone. It had been exposed by an old man. Just like a festering wound needs clear air on it, I had needed to see it for what it was. I needed help and had received it. I had been made vulnerable and survived it.

I peeled myself up from my cozy nest and stretched until I felt I could walk with a normal gait—as normal as my throbbing pinky toe would allow. I made myself a breakfast of instant oatmeal and stood looking out over the scattered hills, the sun peering just above them, while Red Bull and Eric slowly stirred in their own shelters. It was a quiet moment, not because there weren't noises around me; there was a harmony of birds singing their morning songs, campsite sounds, and the wind in the trees, and yet, it was still a quiet moment. My soul was quiet, nothing but a whisper inside.

*What is it like on those hilltops? Under those distant trees?* In the hush of a present mind, I was connected to the voice that only came when I slowed and quieted myself. It was that same internal guide that had led me to a weather-worn archway at the base of Springer Mountain.

I left the trailhead on a high, feeling open in a way I couldn't remember feeling in any part of my former life. I was connected to this experience, connected to the trail, to a population of people who were all fighting their own battles, struggling in their own ways.

Red Bull, Eric, and I shared stories, jokes, and conversations followed by long, comfortable silences as we hiked. I found myself laughing from my gut, not my mind, and thinking deeply without judgment. I spent time allowing myself to hear the sounds of the forest and feel the air on my face. I gazed at the textures around me and wondered at their beauty and complexity. And in a moment of peaceful euphoria, I stubbed my right foot on a root and sucked in a sharp, toothy inhale through a blinding bolt of pain rushing from my pinky toe to my brain.

Internally, the being that I call Ryan was as well as he had ever been. But externally—my beaten and bruised body, my raw hips and shoulders, and more than any other part of me, my right pinky toe were sending warning signals to my brain that no amount of walking meditation could cover. The command center in my skull was taking those signals and doing the thing it was supposed to do, communicating them back to me in the form of very loud thoughts I couldn't ignore.

"Why are you doing this to me, Ryan?"

"I'm not trying to hurt you, Body."

"We're supposed to avoid pain, you know."

"It will get better. I promise."

"You're destroying our foot, Ryan. We need this toe."

I couldn't argue with that, nor un-feel these things. I could not tell the biological responses in my brain to stop firing, and I could not simply stop the thoughts that proceeded from those responses from filling my mind. And I knew from my deep dive into self-reflection over the last several months that we are a species whose actions eventually and unequivocally proceed from our thoughts. I was on a collision course with a certain and unavoidable future if I couldn't address the pain in my right toe, and my time on the trail would come to an end nearly two-thousand miles before I wanted it to. And I had no apparent solutions.

"First state line!"

I was struggling deep in these thoughts when Red Bull announced the milestone. I looked up, startled. I hadn't been looking down at anything in particular, just the mental image of my toe exploding in my shoe.

"Scrambler! Where are you, man? We just crossed our first state line!"

Where was I, indeed! I realized in that critical moment that I was not out of solutions. The problem was my screaming foot, and I was still miles off from the next town, but there was nothing I could do about that. I was not facing a problem of pain and the thoughts that arise from pain; I was in a crisis of focus. I wasn't about to lose my toe; that was fear taking over, the thoughts that dominate the mind and steal its perspective and objectivity. I needed to shift them. That shift was right in front of me.

I stopped and took a deep breath. "First state line." Exhale.

I smiled and high-fived Red Bull and allowed myself to feel the real and present excitement of this first small milestone on the trail. And in that moment, all the pain and discomfort I was feeling, the thoughts in my head, my physical exhaustion—for that little moment, it melted away. There was no pain in this moment, because pain, like every other sense, is just a thought, an alarm sent to alert you to something wrong. And like an alarm, I knew I could take notice of what was wrong, then turn it off. The injury hadn't gone away, but once

I focused on something else, it was no longer the loud ringing sound in my head.

"Appreciate the little things." A friend had armed me with this advice before I set out on the trail. That wasn't a new discovery, more a tool to help me stay centered while I was out there. But now, this strategy held a very tangible and practical purpose for me. Focusing on that one small victory was the best pain medicine. Shifting my attention wasn't about ignoring the problem but about realizing if I couldn't solve it in the moment, I could just a bit further down the road. That had the power to keep me going until I could.

From that moment onward, I shifted my preoccupation with constant pain to emphasizing the little accomplishments of the trail: first state line crossing, one hundred total miles hiked, first twenty-mile day. I did this, all the while enduring the most acute, enduring pain I could remember. When I had no apparent victory to celebrate, I found other positive things to hold my attention: the mighty beauty of the mountains, the freshness of the clear air, the trees with their vast canopies to keep the sun's rays above from burning us, and the occasional outcrop of rock that broke the dense forest to allow a bit of sun to warm our faces. I spoke these thoughts out loud and was surprised when my male companions didn't chide me for my corniness but rather joined in as though the same thoughts had been bottled up in their chests.

While searching for positives to train my attention on during my first full day in North Carolina, about a week into the trail, I realized I hadn't made a single phone call to anyone. For days, I had been unable to consider calling anyone, worried they might ask something terrifying, like how I was doing, forcing me to avoid giving them a complete answer. I didn't want to put myself in that position, to either lie and tell them everything was fine or tell the truth, that I felt like any moment a bloody toe was going to burst out the front of my right shoe and was afraid I couldn't do this. But for the first time in several days, I believed I *was* well on my way. I didn't focus on the endpoint, Katahdin—a strategy I had chosen day one. And I was no longer afraid I would never see it.

I hiked a while by myself that day and called my parents. I don't remember much more than their relief I hadn't been eaten by a bear or fallen into a dark crevasse, but I remember the warmth of their voices, warming me better than the sun had that morning. I remembered that this community I was building on the trail was only part of a larger one off of it, one I had needed more than ever in the tumultuous last year.

When I met the woman who was to become my wife, we were finishing our degrees at Ramapo College of New Jersey, mine in Communications and hers in Education. We were both on track, driven, responsible, hard-working, sprinting toward the American Dream. After college, we buried ourselves in that dream with meetings, business trips, and late nights at the office or school dominating our days. We put our noses directly to the grindstone and ground away the days, turning them into weeks, into months, then years. We were securing our future, building our success, laying the foundation for our long-term, bountiful life together. We were so immersed in this vision, we were doing it apart.

Each day, we left in separate cars to our separate jobs that we didn't return home from until late each night at separate times. We never ate together, always at work or dinners in the office. When home, if we had energy left for anything, it was rare to be present with each other, to confide in or to show our love. We would tell the other whatever minimum was required of two married people about the events of our day and then settle into a numb last hour or so of consciousness, gifting any remaining focus to our television or the inbox on our phones.

It wasn't until our last months together that I began to realize how disconnected I had become. In an effort to make my career successes mean something and provide purpose, I had unwittingly disconnected not only from my wife but also from myself.

As a child growing up in rural northern New Jersey, I had practically lived outside, exploring, pushing my limits, finding my strength, and learning my place, which was everywhere. I was a master of the wilds, scaling trees, crossing creeks, and exploring caves, never shying away from any adventure worth having, sometimes to my detriment. I cracked my head open no less than five times as a kid. Even before the wound scabbed over, I was smiling and would soon be at it again. I never worried about the pain and never worried about my next decision. The decision was always an obvious one—see all there was to see. I was free and instinctual, focused only on the step I was taking. At some point, childhood ended. The expectations of the world moved in to take its place, the instinct which had guided me before was gone, and all I could focus on were the goals I had set for me.

One day, my wife and I were at our local REI. I noticed a Nalgene water bottle with the Appalachian Trail symbol on it and picked it up, reminded of my youth.

"Tell you what?" I said, "I'm going to hike the Appalachian Trail next year, then we can have kids."

My wife had long wanted to grow our family beyond the two of us, something I couldn't even consider at the time—how could two people who spend so little of their waking life together bring additional lives into the mix? When the topic of kids first came up, it was too early for me, I reasoned, but I believed I would work my way, eventually, into a more stable situation at work. I couldn't see the irony at the time, of doing the same thing I was already doing in hopes of different results. Later, I believed she wanted to bring kids into our lives as a way to repair the things in our relationship that were broken. Only, at the time, I didn't think they were broken, and kids seemed like admitting they were.

My wife said nothing as I held the Nalgene bottle in front of me, a smile on my face to mask the instant regret I felt. I had said those words so casually, as if making a light-hearted joke. For what should have been obvious reasons, my wife did not laugh. That moment would come back to me in the months to come as a true litmus test of the growing divide between us. I had grown so disconnected with her and myself that not only did I not realize how hurtful that statement would be, but I also didn't know that I was, in fact, not joking. There was something so buried deep inside, something I hadn't known since I was young. It would take me another year to realize that something inside me was not something but someone—me.

A few months after the Nalgene bottle incident, my wife asked for a separation, and the most exposed thread of my ready-to-unravel life was yanked free into the wind.

By the time I set out on the AT a year later, I had already done a giant amount of internal work, scraping off layers upon layers of disconnected values I had numbed myself into accepting. The Appalachian Trail, in so many ways, required connection. Each stride called for deliberate focus, lest I trip on a slippery rock or step on a nest of ground hornets. Out there, you could only go as fast as your slowest step, and at that pace, there is no choice but to be aware, tethered to the moment. Each careful step reveals the intricacies of the trail—the best slanted rock to place your foot on, the little stream burbling beside you, the sounds masked by the burbling that you may need to be aware of. There is a constant reminder to stay present and enjoy the moment instead of thinking about the distant future…or the past.

The slow unraveling and rebuilding of myself after my divorce allowed me to see myself in a clearer light. I'd done this. Her and I had built our lives apart, but I hadn't tried to fix it. By the time I knew how bad things were between us, there simply wasn't enough left to build upon. We were two entirely different people, different from each other, different from the people we were when we met, more different than either of us thought we would be by that stage in our lives.

I missed us, those moments with her that were good. More than those, I missed the moments that never made their mark, the ones I'd let fly by unnoticed, the ones I could have had if I'd only slowed down enough to see and listen. I missed all that could have been and all I used to be. That's where so much of my efforts went after the separation, learning how to become that again, to appreciate the little moments and cherish them as much as the big goals, to participate in them fully rather than just more objects to step over.

The day we officially completed the divorce, we sat next to each other outside the courtroom, waiting to be called. We spoke very little, and I remember being in tears saying to her, "I wish you could see me now." I realized as soon as I said that how hard it would be to hear. "*Look how well I'm doing, now that we've been apart*," is not what I meant to convey. I wanted her to know, however painful the last eight months had been, that it had not been in vain, that I was a work in progress, and this was a step along the way I needed to take. And I had changed so much by then. My television was gone, completely. Instead, I would build puzzles at night to engage my brain or read books with the purpose of growing and not numbing. I had systematically removed all the material and mental clutter and was replacing it, piece by piece, with thoughts and habits of value.

I recalled all of this as I walked that first full day in North Carolina. The AT wasn't a product to finish, laborious and long. It wasn't something I was trying to get done. It was something I was doing. At the first century mark, one hundred miles traveled, I stopped with Red Bull and Eric and arranged some stones to form the numbers "100". We smiled, bumped fists, and congratulated each other on the accomplishment. We didn't say much because there wasn't much to say. We didn't think about the twenty left in front of us or the difficulty of arriving at that one. We stayed in the moment and enjoyed it in quiet satisfaction.

Not long after my first phone call on the trail, we came to a creek. We knew it was there long before we saw it by the sound of trickling water, and my inner child ignited as it had anytime I approached a bit of running water, a vista, or any other noteworthy point of interest on the trail. As we approached, I saw the stream tumbling down from higher grade and running close to our path where it leveled out into a small pool before plunging back down, away from the trail. I had seen a few dozen or more creeks, streams, and rivers so far on the trail, each unique. As I took in the view, something particular stood out about this one. A group of oddly-shaped rocks shined in the shallow water, tall and narrow with bright colors along their length. As we drew closer, their true identity caused each of us to shout with excitement. These were not tall glimmering stones, these were aluminum cans, unopened, filled with beer. We all stopped and stared for a minute, as if they were a mirage.

I had heard stories of trail magic—snacks, drinks, and other treats left by trail angels. To actually find it was a lot different than I'd imagined. I'm not sure I completely believed I would experience it, like they were just legends in all the thru-hike books I'd read, like some elaborate joke. When coming face-to-face with my first experience, I had a moment of doubt. Hadn't my parents always told me never to eat something if I didn't know where it came from? This ingrained mistrust of strangers rose to the surface like a bubble from the depths of my past, but once it crested the surface and was illuminated under the careful light of examination, it did what all bubbles eventually do—it popped.

After a moment of looking at each other searchingly, we nodded and each stepped forward, grabbed a can, cracked it, and pressed the spring-cooled contents to our lips. As I write this, I haven't had a sip of alcohol in years, but I still remember this one fondly because of how it came to me.

We stood in the crisp, calf-deep water and raised a toast to our unseen angels—not because they had quenched our thirst, but because they had done something much more powerful. They showed us we were not alone.

# 3

## A MAN AND HIS MASK

Every tool has its application, and every strategy has its limit.

I learned at the end of my first week on the trail that, given enough pain, I did not possess enough focus of mind to dull the pain in my shoe. Silly as it may sound, my right pinky toe was proving to be an irrefutable and present problem. There was simply an upper limit to my ability to focus elsewhere. The rest of me had become much quieter, and in that quiet, the screaming of my toe grew to fill my existence. I tried everything to alleviate it. I shifted how I walked many times, doing pedal contortions within my shoes to no benefit and the occasional detriment. I attempted small sections walking backward. I changed socks, doubled my socks, went sockless. I tried taking frequent breaks, soaked my toe in streams, massaged it, heated it by the flame. I taped it to my other toes, walked on my right heel, and at one point, began kicking the point of my right foot into nearby objects just for the few seconds of dullness that came before the inevitable agony. The toe refused to stop hurting.

I had spent considerable time comparing options in the hiking footwear section of my local outdoor outfitters before selecting the ones I now wore. I wore them around the store for a good ten minutes, lunging, hopping about, and coming to abrupt stops like a baby gazelle, all the things I read that I should do before purchasing and wearing them out. They were perfect in every sense that I could detect—waterproof but breathable, flexible but durable, great traction, and more importantly, very comfortable...for about the first five miles. Now, they were a constant misery.

The rest of me had adjusted to life on the trail, but with every step, my toe shouted that it didn't matter how well the rest of me was doing, he was going to be quitting soon if something didn't give.

We had stopped to camp near Long Branch Shelter, and only 7.2 miles separated us from Winding Stair Gap, where we could catch a shuttle to Franklin, North Carolina. Through gritted teeth, I reasoned I would search the town for some solution to my problem. If I could not find one, I would be forced to make devastating plans.

Arriving in Franklin, we followed our noses to Motor Company Grill for lunch and to celebrate Red Bull's 27th birthday. It was the only activity capable of keeping me from race-hobbling to the most important building for me in that town—Outdoor 76. I had no idea what I would be looking for to save me, some type of magic hiker Band-Aid, socks, or a glue I could use to protect the shape of my right pinky toe from the shape of my shoes? Reading thru-hiking guides, I was aware of a product called Second Skin, but I had no confidence that it would fix my problems when my first skin and the inside of my shoe seemed to be in constant battle. But I was willing to try anything, however simple, outlandish, and unlikely. With no idea where to start looking, I stepped up to the counter and did my best not to sound desperate as I described my plight to the young man behind the register.

"Let me see it," was all he said, a smirk on his face that I wasn't sure I liked the portents of. Did this guy have something against thru-hikers and relish seeing them in agony? Or was he preparing himself to tell me what he already knew and what I was ready to believe, that I had suffered a rare but unfortunate malady called Hiker Toe, and there was no hope; I could either remove the toe or leave the trail.

I gingerly removed the shoe and much more gingerly removed the thick sock, revealing a twice-sized pinky toe, angry and red, with a mix of blood and other fluids seeping out of it.

"That's what I figured," said the smirking clerk.

"Hopeless?" I asked with a nervous chuckle.

"Hopeless? Nah, you'll be fine, but whoever helped you pick those out sure didn't do you any favors." He gestured toward my shoes. "They're a full two sizes too small."

I couldn't help but feel slightly insulted by the clerk's nonchalance towards my predicament, but the feeling was quickly replaced by an immense feeling of encouragement. The clerk was right about two things. Me and the smallest toe on my right foot had been in "hiker hell," and the trail runners were two sizes too small, a fact that seemed so obvious as soon as he said it, I wanted to find the nearest stream to drown myself in.

But they hadn't been undersized when I purchased them, the clerk explained to me, saving me a small amount of embarrassment. "The miles of climbs and descents made your feet swell," he went on. "And when feet swell, they swell in every direction, including sideways. Your pinky toe did exactly what you would have done—tried to escape."

The redness in my cheeks abated a small amount, but not entirely. The clerk was wrong about one thing—no one else had caused this but me. I hadn't asked for help at the store in the first place, a thing I could have done at the REI I used to gear up, or before starting the hike by reading about choosing shoes on any of the forums I was a part of, or inquiring at the previous trail town, Hiawasse. But I didn't do any of those things. I had slipped back into my tried-and-true stance of doing everything myself and had nearly done myself in.

"Not even you are tough enough to bear that burden for 2,200 miles, though you gave it your best shot," said the clerk as I contemplated how simple and potentially costly of a mistake this had been.

The remark "Not even you are tough enough..." stuck in my mind like a splinter. This man didn't know me from the hundreds of other thru-hikers who stumbled before him each season. Yet, in ten minutes of chatting with me, rather than thinking of me as a poor idiot, he thought I was a tough guy... or at least someone trying to be tough. I thought about this as I browsed various replacement shoes. It was not a first-time label, nor something I didn't already know about myself. During the exploration of myself in the wake of divorce, I had come across many mentions of a flaw so often found, mostly, in men, that it had a term—mask of masculinity. The term is pretty self-explanatory, but all the problems it can cause are not so easily detected and even less quickly cast aside. My own particular brand of it often led me to avoid asking for help, even in serious situations, rather than chance the risk of being perceived as someone who needed help—you know, like… every real person on the planet!

As ridiculous as it sounds reading it in black and white, it's a defect that has caused me some of my greatest heartaches. During my marriage, I spent so much energy building a life that looked successful, that my marriage was lost in the rubble of that successful-looking life. Everyone would pat me on the back and tell me what a great guy I was for doing so much, but lost in the shuffle was the fact that my life, my partnership, had very serious problems hiding behind the pristinely painted walls of the perfect home we'd made together. When my life fell apart, and my wife and I made the decision to end our marriage, I didn't tell my family for over a month. I felt like such a failure, and admitting it would do to my masculinity-masked mind a far worse thing—I would *look* like a failure. When I finally reached out to meet and tell my older brother, before I could say anything, he slid a book across the table toward me and said, "Ryan, I don't know what's going on in your life, but I want you to read this."

It was a simple thing, just a book about being mindful and intentional, but the effect of being given it floored me. Two realizations gripped me by the heart: one, that the mask I was wearing was only for me, like a blanket against a grim reality…and I wasn't fooling anyone; and two, I didn't need to—my brother, my family, the people closest in my life, these people already knew something was wrong. Something had changed in my communication or my personality, or any of a hundred other little ways, and my family was there to help. I wasn't a failure. I was one of a community of people who had made mistakes, small ones and life-changing ones, and we were all in this together.

# 4

## THE JOY FOR THE PAIN

I left the outdoor outfitters store in Franklin with two pairs of boots in my hands, one worn down by nearly two hundred miles of rocks and dirt, weather and blood, the other new, padded and stuffed with paper, protected by a thick, shiny cardboard box. I sat on the curb, ten feet from the entrance, and pulled my stinking, sweaty socks back on, slid my feet into their new homes, and tied them tight. The relief was immediate. My toes spread out as though sprawling back on a new oversized couch, and as I took long, lunging steps up and down the sidewalk, my weight shifted comfortably without pressure or pain. My pinky toe stopped screaming and exhaled its former discomfort out of the shoes and into the atmosphere.

Inspired by Tommy's shakedown service from a few days before, I decided to perform a miniature version of my own, albeit without the benefit of expert guidance. Examining each of the items I brought, I was surprised and not entirely unproud of myself to find I was using all but one of them. My inflatable pillow was the only thing I sent back. It didn't take up much space when deflated, but a little more than a week on the trail,

I realized it just wasn't comfortable to lay your head down on a sack of air, contradicting the sole purpose of a pillow.

We took the shuttle back from Franklin, and when we rejoined the trail the next morning, it was like taking my first steps again. The previously ever-present worry of whether I could handle the next set of miles melted away, a seemingly distant memory. I was alive to the world again, beyond the confines of pain, both here and focused. I regained the ability to be eager for what came next and appreciated when it did. The smell of pine needles and the beauty of the many mountain vistas, the simple joy that a sip of cool water could bring—these were all gifts again, instead of reminders of what I would soon be missing.

As I enjoyed my mental and spiritual return to the trail, I felt a rising appreciation for the hardships that came before. I actually found myself thanking the trail for the pain it had caused, for the contrasting gratefulness I now felt. Then I was taken further back. I felt a new warmth for my family and all those who had supported me through the divorce and all the lessons learned from that experience. Perhaps I hadn't fully shed my mask of masculinity, and maybe I never would. But that little moment of vulnerability, the simple act of seeking aid from another, that was something I could and needed to build on.

The next several days were a breaking in of my new boots. First was a 21.2-mile effort which caused my feet to swell back up as predictably full as they had before, but my two-sizes-larger toe box swallowed them without any rubbing or other conflict with the wall of canvas. We made it to Wesser Bald that day and Sassafras Gap the next. The weather cooperated, as did my body, feeling recovered and stronger. For the first time, I felt I was living up to my trail name, Scrambler.

At Fontana Dam, just before entering the Great Smoky Mountains National Park, I took a lot of photos and thought a lot of my dad, a Dam Surveyor for much of his career. Out of reflex, I began to send some of the shots of the dam to him in a text but stopped. I imagined how much more meaningful it would be to sit with him later and look at the pictures together, to hear firsthand what he would have to say about them. And I knew he would say plenty. Growing up, anytime a dam was spotted, he would rattle off obscure facts and terminology as though everyone present was interested and understood what he was saying, a fact that made me smile as I stood there beside one without him.

The only hiccup during that stretch of days was a close encounter with a rattlesnake in the middle of the trail. Red Bull had just stepped over the camouflaged creature in front of me when the rattle sounded, sending me into an acrobatic performance I didn't know I was capable of. We thought about grabbing a stick and guiding the serpent off the trail but opted for caution over valor and just slowly skirted around it, thankful no muscles were pulled or venom kits opened.

A few days later, we set up camp at Double Spring Gap Shelter only 2.7 miles from Clingman's Dome, a destination twice circled on my trail map. The tallest part of the AT, Clingman's Dome offers some of the furthest vistas on the entire trail. With those warm expectations in my mind, I sat outside my tent that evening, staring off into the sunset until the colors faded from orange to purple, then to an inky blue field of stars. I stared into that dark expanse full of distant twinkles for a while before retiring to my tent and writing a brief entry in my journal which began with, "I'll make this short because my body is very tired…" and ended with, "…Tomorrow will be a good day." I fell asleep certain of that fact. I woke up less so.

"Tomorrow" was decidedly not a "good day." After closing my journal, I had barely shuttered my eyes for the night before being assaulted by a sharp onset of nausea. Things escalated quickly from there, including multiple trips out into the cold night for violent hurling followed by very little sleep that came only in the form of sickness-induced nightmares.

I had just begun to feel like I could fall into a deep sleep when the sun came up the next morning. My slurred speech to my hiking mates, what sounded in my head like, "I will be staying in bed a few extra hours," came out more like, "Stay bed, more sleep…" To my best recollection, they gave me their wishes for improved health and informed me they would not be waiting.

From the rest of that morning, I only remember falling asleep and waking every fifteen minutes or so, my mouth feeling like cotton and my stomach ready to wretch again at any fleeting thought of food. Each time I woke, I sipped small amounts of water. Every few wakes, I'd try to nibble something small, each time learning the better of it. It wasn't until late that morning that I was lucid enough to realize it might be better to let the food wait, or I would never absorb what little water I was getting down, approaching serious dehydration. Within an hour of skipping the nibbles and focusing only on the sips, I felt like I had been administered a steroid shot.

A few hours later, I was well enough to scold myself for why I was sick in the first place. It wasn't a stomach bug or anything else you might dread on the trail, like Norovirus or tick-borne pathogens such as Lyme Disease or Rocky Mountain Spotted Fever. I was simply dehydrated. With my new boots, I was putting in big miles day after day, caught up in the refreshed experience of it all—the sights, sounds, conversations, and all the reflections they brought. I had spent so much of my focus on what was playing out all around me that I'd created another problem to contend with, one that ironically, I had previously struggled against—an extreme focus on myself and the pain I'd been experiencing. With my focus shifted outside of myself, I hadn't afforded enough of it for the simple act of drinking water.

I continued to sip slowly, and I continued to feel better in small increments until the early afternoon, so I decided to venture out to avoid losing the entire day of planned mileage. My feet no longer hurt, but that wasn't the only effect my new boots provided me, that day. Wearing them in my present condition felt like putting a thin wrapping around the cinder blocks that replaced my feet. Those heavy blocks took me to another milestone that afternoon, the second century mark, 200 miles on the trail. I stopped and forced myself to celebrate, though nothing about me felt like it.

After documenting the 200-mile crossing with a photo, I continued the slow, somewhat delirious 2.7-mile slog to the top of Clingmans Dome. By the time I arrived at the top, I barely had enough energy left to lift my eyes, but as soon as I did, every heave of a step getting there became worth it.

Before me was a seemingly endless painting. Deep green trees disappeared into a blue-green ridge. Behind that was a backdrop of further ridges in misty blue, which faded almost imperceptibly into a slate-blue sky beyond. It was as close to staring out towards the end of the earth as I had ever felt. My spirits were lifted by the seemingly infinite beauty. My feet were lighter, reduced from cinder blocks to normal-sized bricks. Looking further down the trail, I felt another jolt of optimism when I recalled that I would be heading downhill for a considerable distance from this tallest point.

I pulled myself away from the awe of Clingman's Dome, and by the time I had reached the halfway point down its slopes, the trail had thoroughly reacquainted me with the fact that downhill hiking was not much easier than up. Instead of an endless set of steps, it was a slow, jolting fall, each pace a shock to every muscle and joint. Not long after reaching the bottom, I was forced to contemplate how much further I could safely hike into that day, though there was plenty of day left. That was when I stumbled upon another Trail Angel, or rather, he stumbled upon me.

At Newfound Gap, a spot where the trail comes out to a road and a parking lot gives access to day-hikers looking to enjoy the incredible views of that area, I took advantage of a short rock wall separating the parking area from the overlook. Unsure whether I had it in me to continue, I decided I would take a short nap. It was very short.

"Hello there!" called a man from a distance.

I opened my eyes and greeted him with as much energy as my current state could afford, a simple nod and an attempt at words I don't think made it past my lips.

"Are you alright?" he asked. "Do you need water?"

"No," I managed. "I have water…thanks. I'm just…" I held up a finger "…getting over something." I gestured to my stomach.

He nodded. "Here, take these."

"No—" I began to say.

"Please," he held up a hand. "I want you to take them. I'm almost done, and I brought way more snacks than I need. You'll be saving me from worrying about the calories. Come on, it's ok to get a little help now and then."

Right… Help… Yes.

"Thank you." I stood and took the bag which contained peanut M&Ms, Gatorade, and potato chips.

"Go ahead, eat up," he encouraged me, and once he had said that, I realized through the fog of fatigue that filled my brain that I had just entered another problem.

Without saying it, he was announcing that he wasn't leaving, not yet. I didn't want him to leave, necessarily; that wasn't the problem. I didn't want him to see what would likely become of the food in the moments after I ate it.

I could barely remember what day it was, much less think of some graceful way out of the predicament, so I twisted the top off the Gatorade and took a sip. The orange liquid, I reasoned, would be the least caustic to my finicky guts. I felt the cool liquid coat my esophagus and stomach, and a fire ignited inside me. Far from causing further internal upset, every drop of that precious liquid instantly voyaged to different parts of my body and set off little explosions of energy.

Emboldened and suddenly famished, I set the Gatorade aside and tore open the bag of chips. I collected two of the small oval objects, the smallest amount my newfound voracious appetite would allow, and placed them in my mouth. I crunched and swallowed and became at once larger and stronger, yet somehow lighter and less of a burden on my legs. With every bite, my feet grew lighter still.

By the time I reached the peanut M&Ms, I had no reserve left in me and took down the entire snack-size bag in one gulp. The man didn't seem the least bit surprised, nor to even notice it. During the five minutes of our encounter, in which I ate the entire offering, the man stood there telling me about how he had thru-hiked the AT many years before and was only there now to share the view with his family. He loved running into thru-hikers and said it was the next best thing to being out on the trail himself. His trail name was Mountaineer.

I thanked him for his generosity and turned back to the trail, stumbling into the afternoon, myself headed north and Mountaineer back to his people. I felt like a renewed person, filled with so much more than energy—I was unstoppably grateful, the kind that makes you smile without trying, even when you're alone. I couldn't stamp down this happiness, even though I knew I was going to be many miles short of the day's goal.

I thought about Mountaineer the rest of that leg and while setting up camp that evening, how I wouldn't have met him and received his kind gift had I not decided to hike that day. There had been no better excuse than the one I had to stay in my tent and nurse my roiling stomach and disappointed feelings. But something within had made me stand up, and once I stood, that something caused me to take another step, then another. It was by all metrics a below-average day, finishing a paltry thirteen miles. But I recovered during my hike, and perhaps because of it.

In my past, I might have decided to call that day in, to stay home and avoid the office, lest people see me not at my best. I don't know exactly what was different about the Ryan of now compared to the Ryan before, but there was something freeing about just having showed up, even poorly.

The next day was a very good day, decidedly the most beautiful miles I had seen on the trail. I felt better the moment I opened my eyes, still tired and a little weak as I stretched and breakfasted, but well on my way to being fully recovered. I stepped onto a stretch of trail I didn't know I was at the beginning of.

It was like nothing I had ever seen. Rich moss clumped in soft mounds, hugging both sides of the two-foot-wide path of dirt. The path itself looked perfectly manicured, as if little gnomes must have lived in the forest there, whose sole joy was to keep the trail tidy and well-edged. The moss continued in tufts and tiny hillocks into a dense forest of bare trunks, rising like the long stems of antlers from the head of a buck, splitting and fanning out into branches once they reached far above the ground. High above, a thick canopy burst into deep green leaves, needles, and cones. There was a hush in that section of the trail, and I could not decide whether it was coming from the dampening nature of the moss or the stillness of my soul.

I walked along, not aware of how fast or slow I was moving, of how long my strides were, or how far I had gone. I was in that rare state of being somewhere between completely present and not present at all, entirely aware of everything around me and not consciously aware of anything, least of all myself. I was Ryan, Scrambler, thru-hiker, and at the same time, I might as well have been the breeze overhead, the leaves fluttering, or the tufted moss.

I hiked from 8:00 that morning to 4:00 in the afternoon with very little awareness of the passing time. It was only when I arrived at Cosby Knob Shelter that I realized I had hiked twenty miles. That evening, I thought again about how I wouldn't have had that experience had I not gotten sick and had I not decided to trudge on through it anyway. I would have still hiked the same path, but I wouldn't have begun it the way I did, right at the moment when the trail became so pristine. Mostly, I wouldn't have been in the space of mind, one of stark and raw appreciation, a mindset that had allowed me to experience the beauty exactly the way I needed to, the way it deserved to be appreciated. Before exhaustion overtook me that night, I smiled and thought about how sometimes it is the very worst of times in our lives that put us on course for the very best ones.

# 5

## A VIEW TO SELF

My eyes fluttered open at the first peek of light hitting the east-facing side of my tent. I was instantly fully awake, something I'd noticed a few days into this hike. There wasn't the same three to five minutes of coaxing myself to engage, with a long, intense drowsiness followed by the many small increments of getting out of bed. On the trail, I would go from being fast asleep to being awake and alert. Falling asleep was also different than before; most nights it was as simple as deciding to. I would use the last of my energy blowing warm breaths into my thin air mattress until it was thick enough that I could no longer feel what was beneath, lay down, close my eyes, and wake the next morning without recalling a dream.

The energizing beauty of the twenty miles from the day before and the prospect of my destination that day had me getting out of bed even more quickly than the usual trail morning. I was nearing the end of the Smokies, and though I would be leaving a part of my heart in those misty mountains, I was ready for a new stage of the trail. I would soon be entering the fabled lush green tunnels and blue ridges of northern North Carolina and Virginia. I was also, perhaps even more, excited about reaching the first major destination outside of the Smokies: Max Patch.

I set off after a quick breakfast, hoofing it out of the official boundaries of the Great Smoky Mountains before pausing at 11 A.M., making eleven miles—my first 11-by-11 morning—halting only for a brief rest and a few bites at a saddle on Flat Ridge. The trail was for me making my goal that day, a hike as opposed to scrambling or climbing. The weather provided me with a full day of clear blue, late spring skies, which shined through the canopy above and greeted me warmly at every open vista. During the stretch, I had caught up with Red Bull and Eric for the first time since they'd left camp the morning I was sick. After saying our hellos, I asked about their plans for the day. "Max Patch," was their two-word answer in unison. I confirmed with a smile and nod, adding that camping there was something I'd been looking forward to since planning to hike the AT. Unsurprisingly, each shared the same with me. We made a pact that we wouldn't stop until we reached our destination. Though it would become my longest day of miles up to that point, never once did any of us mention stopping.

Late in the afternoon, by the time the sun began to paint the first streaks of pink shades into the blue expanse, I had hiked a whopping twenty-four miles, my longest single day of hiking so far on the trail. We emerged from a thick forest edge at the base of a gentle climb, and the landscape slowly revealed its rare beauty. With every step, the open ridge of grass and wildflowers rose above the encircling trees until we stood at the crest of the most unhindered viewscape I had experienced on the trail, the bald known as Max Patch.

Max Patch, just beyond the Great Smoky Mountains, stands at an elevation of fifty feet above the nearest treetops and about 4,617 feet above the rest of the world. It was a sight unlike any other. Expansive and green to its edges, standing at the top and looking down at your feet, you might have felt like you were on a grassy hilltop, but looking out in any direction, there was something fantastical about the feeling it gave you, like you were on an island floating in the clouds. The lush green ran in every direction toward infinity like the blue horizon of the ocean seen from a boat with no shore in sight. It was both beautiful and unsettling all at once. One wrong step, and you might fall into the open sky, so it seemed.

The sun began to set and cast a soft orange glow on the world, and the few passing gray clouds bathed in light gave way to a soft watercolor pink. To the north and west, stark purpled mountains rose upward into the warm glowing sky, while to the east and south, the land slowly disappeared into the shadows cast by the peaks and ridges I had hiked for the last seventeen days. I stood tall on the grassy knoll and felt myself become a part of that shadow.

I lay down for the night in my sleeping bag, looking out the open flap I had positioned to take in the slowly dimming sunset, reflecting on how just a few days earlier, I had been so close to hanging up my boots (literally) and going home. It was impossible to look at that sky and not feel the gratitude I hadn't. I took a deep, cool breath and thanked the first stars in the sky that I had made it to this place.

The next morning, I emerged from my tent and stepped around to the opposite side where a scene just as unique as the evening before was beginning to form. The sun announced its rise first on the highest peaks to the northeast, burning their tips like candlewicks before marching down the slopes, valleys, and thick forests to then bathe the little towns and meadows in golden light, burning away the shadows that blanketed the mountains and myself the night before. The tents of other campers rustled, and the morning flowers of the meadow were open, inviting bees and butterflies to visit them again, and a chorus of different birdsongs served as a gentle call to the late risers. I just stood there, taking in all the warmth of the experience, breathing deeply and thinking as little as possible except for the small thoughts I could form about what I was seeing.

When the air had begun to warm and the sky was blue again, I looked down, not at my feet, but in joyful sadness knowing the experience of that sunrise was over, and my day would soon begin. It would remain one of the fondest memories of my time on the trail.

That day, I moved a little more slowly than the day before, a little more reflective, a little more drawn into myself. I thought about all the sunsets and rises I'd missed in my rush to "be successful". A few miles into the day, I sniffed involuntarily, and my breath caught in my chest. I felt my face flush, and the rims of my eyes stung for just a moment, and then I stopped and tried to take a deep breath, but it betrayed me. Something broke open inside, and I began crying. I tried to stop, but that only made it come harder, like patching a hole in a dam ready to burst. So, I relinquished it and sobbed, not sure what exactly I was sobbing about. I cried and smiled, cried and shouted, and cried and laughed at how ridiculous I must have looked, then cried some more. I cried until the whole contents of whatever I had been holding back, holding inside, had emptied itself from me.

I felt something switch, and I thought I was done crying, but I wasn't. The tears continued, but they were different. They were just as overwhelming as the ones before, but these tears were from something or many things I could feel and see— the sunset and sunrise, the twenty miles the day before, the man who had given me his bag of snacks; I saw the clerk at the counter in the outfitters store and felt the relief in my right pinky toe; I remembered receiving my trail name, Scrambler, and standing before the worn stone archway with the red sign and white letters beside it. I felt those and a hundred other moments as I cried, and I cried knowing that I would have a thousand more before this hike was over. Suddenly, like a rainstorm blowing through, I stopped crying, wiped my face, and stepped onward without any shame.

I stepped for twenty miles that day, feeling lighter in my soul but gradually heavier in my boots. The last two days of twenty-plus miles were starting to take their toll. It was no small relief when I spotted the first sign of the destination I had been moving toward: a white and blue reflective Appalachian Trail Conservancy sign off to the side which read, "Appalachian Trail Community, Hot Springs, North Carolina."

Hot Springs, I came to learn, is a true "trail town." The AT runs directly through the heart of it, along the small-town main street, before a train track and a bridge across the French Broad River marks the edge of civilization, depositing you back into the wild. I was not quite ready for that yet. In fact, I wouldn't be for more than 36 hours.

I decided to take my first "zero" in Hot Springs, a day of no hiking miles. I hadn't planned to, but my body had responded to an information sign declaring the town as the only place on the trail with natural hot springs. There was almost nothing that sounded better to my aching muscles and limbs than to soak in a spring of hot mineral water—almost nothing... because there was always one thing that sounded better than any other way of passing time—eating.

My mind made up, I followed the signs to the Hot Springs Spa and Resort, the only actual place in town where you could safely and legally access the steaming natural water. Red Bull and I were able to secure a room for the night and got ourselves cleaned and dressed in clothes that didn't smell like weeks of sweat. There was something unsettling about seeing my soiled brown and very callused feet against the pristine white tile floor of my room's shower. It was disorienting, like I was looking at two very different realities and wasn't sure which one was normal. After eighteen days on the trail, the concept of dirt had changed somewhat in my mind. I wouldn't say I had come to like it, but it no longer felt like a sin to be "dirty," something that needed to be remedied as soon as possible.

Once I was sufficiently clean and smelling like I belonged in society again, I fought the urge to rush to an early dinner and instead found my way to the spa where I soaked for some time, listening to the gurgling warm water and hoping it would coax my tight and sore muscles free. When the sounds of my stomach exceeded the ones from the water, I dried off and dressed for the evening. I walked the town's short main street lined on one side with a few charming shops, then followed my nose into a local steakhouse and pub. There were quite a few thru-hikers in the establishment, an atmosphere like a high school reunion but where everyone present liked each other.

The next day was a complete zero day, not a single mile hiked, and I felt zero guilt about it. Having gotten what I needed from the hot springs, I moved my belongings to Elmer's Sunnyside, a hostel in town, then enjoyed breakfast at the Hot Springs Diner where I ate their last two remaining cinnamon rolls. After eating my fill, I did some laundry at the town's only laundromat, nothing more than a tiny building with two washers and dryers, then resupplied at the town outfitter. That night, I did my best to fill my seemingly unfillable stomach with a full rack of ribs, complete with sides, and two desserts—a chocolate peanut butter pie and an old-fashioned brownie sundae.

The next day, though coming down hard with rain, I decided to stick to my plans and get back on the trail. My hiking mates stayed behind, and that was just fine. I knew I would want to join back up with other hikers at some point, but I felt confident I would know when the time was right.

Spending time in the relative luxury of the accommodations the last couple of nights had reminded me of life off the trail. As I hiked with nothing keeping me company besides my thoughts, I found myself thinking about why things had fallen apart in my marriage—how I had begun to feel married to our house and goals, all the material and financial parts of our life, and no longer to the woman I had fallen in love with. Our relationship had turned into one of just living together, contributing efforts and funds toward the expenses of our separate lives and goals.

She had decided to move into an apartment while we were in our separation, and I remember just standing there alone in our empty home. All I could think was how big it was, how all my time had gone into being able to afford it but rarely ever enjoy it. Even then, with my marriage falling apart, my priorities were still arrow-focused on my career. It was a couple weeks after she moved into her own place when she called me. I was in my car, driving in heavy traffic home from some meeting or function for work, a usual evening for me at the time. I remember having just screamed at the gridlock traffic in front of me when my phone rang. I picked up and don't remember what either of us said to begin the call, I only remember her asking the question she had called to ask.

"Do you think we should give it another try?"

There was a long pause, then I heard words in my voice say, "No. I don't think we can work this out."

I know I finished driving and parked my car somehow, but I don't remember any of it. I only remember laying on my bed crying that night and long into the morning, knowing that despite all the work I had put into building this life, I was a failure. I had failed in building the one thing that it was all for.

It was about a month later, around the time I met with my brother and told him about the impending divorce, that I decided I was going to make another major change—I was going to leave my career of ten years, the very thing I had spent years in college for, leave the thing society told me was the ultimate goal in life. I knew I had not been happy in my career for a long time and in that exposed state, realized that a long time also meant never. I had found myself many times struggling to find any purpose, meaning, or joy in the work I was doing or any real alignment with that work and the core values of who I was. More than anything else, though, I was simply moving at a pace that never allowed for self-reflection, to check in and ask those critical questions: "Who am I? What do I think about all this going on around me? What should I do about it?" I had been driving ninety down the highway of my life, white-knuckled, eyes trained on the little white stripes… never seeing all the beautiful trees and towns I was passing.

The deciding moment for me was while reading the book my brother had slid across the table at our meeting. The entire book was one new perspective after another, the kind of thing you experience and immediately regret not having known your entire life. But there was one particular concept in that book that punched me right in the stomach. It was such a simple thought: just because you had always been a certain way, didn't mean you had to stay that way.

I knew I would need time to figure out what the next part of my journey was going to be. What better way than an actual journey? I thought about that Nalgene bottle at REI. As soon as I remembered the words "Appalachian Trail," I knew without any doubt that was what I wanted to do. And I think I subconsciously had known it then, too. So, I walked into work the next day and had an open and honest discussion about all of this with my boss. She wasn't mad or upset. She was more envious than anything. A few months later, I officially put in a four-month notice.

As I ruminated about all these events on the trail, feeling all the freedom that had come with the decision and with the clarity of seeing everything in hindsight, I had the realization that it wasn't actually being on the trail that made me truly free.

I don't want anyone to read this and believe that they have to hike the Appalachian Trail in order to find themselves. It also wasn't ending my marriage or leaving my career, though I do believe those things were a necessary part of my journey of change and rediscovery. The true key was the mindset I learned to adopt, one amplified by the trail. It was the ability to appreciate the current moment, the willingness to be in it, and taking it in at the speed the moment required. I don't know if I had known and applied that mindset earlier in my life, whether I would have saved my marriage or my career, or if it would have led me to never pursue them in the first place. But one thing I felt confident about as I put Hot Springs, North Carolina, further and further to the south of me was that I had needed to break up the life I was living in order to see all the pieces of me and begin to understand them again. Only then could I begin to put them back together in a better form. It was a humbling thought to admit and one that had me fending off those old reflexive feelings of failure as I walked. As fate would have it, an equal and opposite buoying experience was waiting for me a few days outside Hot Springs.

I left Spring Mountain Shelter feeling content but somewhat solemn for all the contemplation about my past life the day before. I had a decent day of hiking—beautiful scenery, about 16 miles, nothing extraordinary but respectable. That afternoon, about a quarter of a mile before reaching my shelter for the evening, I crossed the 300-mile mark of the trail. I was alone. I stopped and took a few breaths, recalling what I had read in forums and books about this point on the trail, that this was the first great filter, the line about 50 percent of aspiring thru-hikers would never see the other side of. I gathered enough small stones to spell out "300" in large numerals on the side of the trail, something to look at and form a lasting memory of, another of the many little moments I celebrated as I went.

It was both humbling and emboldening being in the company of hikers who had made it this far and knowing it would only get harder. It had not been easy. As I thought ahead to the more than 1,800 miles left, for a brief moment, I wondered whether there was real value in what I was doing, great enough to equal the hardship suffered, the money spent, and all the time invested. Pre-trail Ryan would have weighed those thoughts very carefully and would have been forced, by the very nature that made him so calculated, to choose every step that took him on the course toward his "American dream."

But standing three hundred miles from Springer Mountain after hiking for three weeks, this work-in-progress version of me knew there was immense value in enduring hardship, pushing myself toward what I believed were my limits, and seeing myself burst through the other side of them. Money was only a tool, a very useful one, but nothing more than that—a thing to bring value, not a value in itself. If my life choices were already bringing me fulfillment, why should I want any more money than I needed? And time—the concept of wasting time doing anything you love was no more real than the others. If the thing you are doing is giving you meaning and purpose, time spent doing it is never wasted.

On that long trail, hundreds of miles from my comfort zone, I was finding more meaning and purpose than I had anywhere else in the last ten years.

# 6

## PITTER PATTER, MOMENTS MATTER

Every day seemed to provide a new realization about how different "life on the trail" was from what I previously thought of as "life". Obvious things like not having a shower were present, but the implications of this reality forced into your thoughts things like what it means to be clean, concepts of what far and fast are in reference to distance traveled, and what actually is an inconvenience versus what is not. The longer I was on the trail, the more my perspective was forced to change about these and many other topics most of society takes for granted.

Something that hadn't changed was the fact that waking up to the sound of rain made it measurably more difficult to get out of bed, though for very different reasons. I lay there contemplating this at Jerry's Cabin Shelter as the gods of the trail watered the world around me. I thought about how back in the "real world" on a rainy morning, I would lay half awake, the cares of the previous day and the upcoming one drowned away in the soft wet symphony. I let my mind stay in that place for a long spell before returning to the trail, where rain in the morning meant extra effort, a hundred extra little movements that I would have to make to stay dry. I needed to protect the contents of my pack…and my skin, if I was lucky. More than a small part of me considered staying exactly where I was, pretending that I didn't have mileage goals or a life to eventually get back to, or at least one to rebuild.

I forced my eyes open with a sigh, resigned to the fact that I didn't know when the rain would stop. If I lay waiting, I could likely be waiting long into the afternoon, days even. I packed my supplies, shaking each with one hand while using my rain jacket as a limp umbrella with the other, coaxing everything back into their right place. After I had done a poor job of packing everything dry, I was back on my way with a few cold bites in my stomach. This was a repeat of the previous day and the past few mornings. As unpleasant as it was, after an entire morning of downpour, the fourth in a row and about seven miles of hiking, I knew I had made the right decision.

I finished a steep descent down the eastern slopes of Snake Den Ridge, during which I saw no snakes at all, likely due to the heavy rain, then began an equally sharp climb back upward on Flint Mountain. By the time I reached the top of that first ascent, I had not found any flint either and began to wonder if the whole naming convention for geological features was a sham. I stopped and sucked down a packet of peanut butter before consulting my trail guide. There was nothing of note for the next several miles except for a scenic vista at Devil Fork Gap, where Devil Fork Road cut along a lower ridge on the other side. I felt confident the naming convention was going to provide at least one more disappointment. Beyond the gap, there was nothing but treed slopes and ridges until my intended destination for the night at Hogback Ridge Shelter.

As the first ridge of Flint Mountain crested and gave way to a new downward slope, I saw a sign that read "Food" with an arrow pointing in a direction off trail. Given my intense hunger, I followed the sign to more signs until I arrived at a random barn in the woods. No other hikers were there, and I wondered if I had been lured off the trail, only to be murdered. Before I found my way to the entrance, a gentleman came out of a nearby house and offered to cook for me. He explained that he was working on getting set up as an official hostel. I didn't ask, but I had the distinct impression that I was his first customer.

About an hour later, not only had I not been murdered, I had eaten and enjoyed a burger, pizza, and Gatorade.

Not long after the experience at the unexpected food stop, I had an equally pleasant surprise. Ending my hike that day at Uncle Johnny's Hostel, I found myself surrounded by thru-hikers I had not met before, all enjoying a respite from the rain. I was going through my pack, drying items with a towel provided by the owner when I heard my name.

"Ryan?" I turned and found Tommy standing at the entrance.

"Tommy!" I called back.

"BAMF," he corrected me.

"BAMF?"

"BAMF. Bad-ss Motherf-cker!" he said, and there was something about hearing this in his French accent that made it more comical than abrasive.

"BAMF," I parroted back, nodding.

"I'll tell you all about it," he said and put an arm around my shoulder, ushering me toward the counter where I would order a cheeseburger, a full pepperoni pizza, and a large Powerade to wash both down.

Tommy had been hiking with a few other thru-hikers putting in massive miles each day. They exclaimed that he was, in fact, a Bad-ss Motherf-cker, and that promptly became his trail name. They explained he should probably abbreviate it due to the number of families on the trail, and thus, Tommy became BAMF.

It was the perfect trail name for him, and hearing him proudly speak the elongated version several times in that way only someone with choppy American English can get away with and not sound like a stereotypical frat jock made it even better. I couldn't help smiling, though considering how the only reason I had caught up with this so-named guy was due to the fact that he had sprained an ankle and was here at this very hostel nursing it back to health. Not very BAMF-ish, I thought, and yet nothing could be more fitting for the goofy guy beside me.

That night at Uncle Johnny's Hostel, I began thinking about meeting up with my family further down the trail, something I had loosely begun planning. I wondered about who would be there. My parents would be, of course, and maybe some more family members. But would I see any other familiar faces? Was the Ryan they thought they knew a person they would want to meet and cheer for? Was I worth driving the few miles out of their way to see me home? I realized, as disappointed as I might be if no one else showed, I couldn't blame anyone. I hardly recognized the man I was just a few months before. I had always been friendly, social, and willing to spend free time with friends and family whenever there was free time. But I was a shell and a shill, so caught up in the game of progress and product that everyone I called "friend" was also playing some part in that game with me. There were very few people I made time for that I cared about for their sake only. I had lost sight of authentic friendship. I had lost sight of the authentic "me".

The next morning, as I put more miles of hiking in the rain behind me, it felt like I was walking home to the person I used to be before I had started playing "the game." Growing up near the Appalachian Trail in New Jersey, I never saw it as anything of any great importance, just the woods I would disappear into for a day. Looking back on those memories, I realized just how far from that trail I had come and how far I had to walk to get back. So much had happened to the Ryan who grew up there. So much had changed, been added to, and been subtracted from. This experience was another of those moments that added or subtracted, and I wondered which it was—was I becoming more or less the real me?

The rain gathered on my mustache and streamed in little spurts into my mouth, and I tasted the salt my skin added to it and smiled. I didn't have to wonder. This experience was both adding and subtracting to Ryan. The experience of life itself, the moments of silence and laughter, the time spent thinking and wondering and not thinking at all were all added. Subtracted from me were the previously held idea of who I was and the belief that my worth was found in a title, a salary, a position of responsibility, or anything that could be purchased by having those things. The scabs that covered the wounds of life were falling away, and under them, I found healthy skin, Ryan's skin, parts of myself I hadn't seen so clearly since trekking into the woods of the Appalachian Mountains of my childhood.

That night in my tent, I thought more about what was being added to my life on the trail. That in itself was something new, something I never would have done before, taking stock of what I was learning. Before, I might have poured over the minutes of a meeting, brushed up on a new product I was selling, gleaned what I could of the people at the company I was going to sell it to—anything and everything to advance my career, make more money, build "more life." Never would I have spent time intentionally doing less and thinking more, thinking about who I was intrinsically, or who I was becoming.

A flood of thoughts flowed from pen to paper as I frantically scribbled eight lessons into my journal, wondering whether I would still agree with them after I was off the trail and whether I would still be the thoughtful person I thought I was becoming. "Slow and steady wins the race," I jotted down first and shook my head at how cliché that immediately sounded. "Get comfortable being uncomfortable," came next, and I tried to picture the man at my local REI in East Hanover, New Jersey who told me this, his face eluding me. Those were both certainly true, but what had I learned? What was from me? Then it came: "You don't need much to live," I scribed. Now we were getting somewhere. "There is beauty in everything if you choose to see it," I wrote next, and a slideshow of recent memories played out in my head, and I smiled and paused, appreciating each one. But there wasn't only beauty out here. "It's easy to psych yourself out," came next, as I recalled the last four days of rain. "All problems are short-lived" and "Patience is a virtue." Both seemed to arrive in rebuttal to each other, though I smirked disappointedly at the last as the most hallmark and borrowed of the bunch. I paused for a moment after that and forced myself not to jot down the several other rapid-fire thoughts that I knew were playing back to me from books or memes, waiting for something to close on that was uniquely my experience. I scanned back through the list of seven lessons and stopped on the word "comfortable." I had thought I was comfortable for a time—in my career, in my marriage, in every step I took toward what I believed I was "supposed" to be doing. I thought I was comfortable knowing that everyone could look at me and say, "he's doing it right." And yet, nothing about my life was comfortable—not the large home which housed my disconnected relationship with my wife, not the successful career to which I gave my every waking energy, not the future I looked toward, the one that saw me pushing harder and harder until I had destroyed everything that made me "me." I was comfortable with the illusion. But that illusion should have been discomforting. So many times, I looked in a mirror and saw the reflection staring back at me as unrecognizable. I should have been alarmed, but each time I told myself I was seeing what I was supposed to be, even though I didn't recognize I had become someone quite different from who I was inside. I had become comfortable with a lie. It was the story I had told myself every day for years. It became all I knew about myself. And doing anything different was dangerous to what I thought I knew.

"8:" I scrawled slowly. "Stepping out of your comfort zone is far greater than the comfort itself."

As soon as I put the pen down, I felt like a fraud. I flushed and began to sweat as if someone might rip the journal from my hands as I lay in my tent and tell me how obvious or foolish or how poorly thought out each of these were. Who was I to be writing down life lessons? And who would I even be sharing these lessons with? I wanted to tear out the page and burn the evidence that such scribblings ever existed. I read back over the list. I believed each but felt so much like an imposter writing them. I grabbed the page as if to tear it out but saw the first half of that page filled with recollections of the day. I couldn't bring myself to destroy those words or spend the effort writing them again on a clean page, so I closed the journal and did my best to pardon myself for thinking so highly of my thoughts to write down takeaways from the trail. No one would read or hear what I had written anyway.

The next morning, rain greeted and ushered me into the day again, and again, I was slow to creep out of my sleeping bag. During that day's hike, I became so frustrated with the constant downpour, I stopped dead in my tracks and clenched my fists and actually stomped the ground…like a child. I didn't say a word, just stood there holding my breath and stomping with fingers tightened into balled fists and straining the muscles in my face and neck until I thought my eyes might pop. Then I let a long exhalation escape my chest and became even more frustrated with myself at having become so angry in the first place. I thought back to lessons two, six, and seven in my journal and how, in the span of a single morning, I had seemingly forgotten them. I was certain then that my suspicions of the previous night were true. I was a fraud and should have torn the page out and buried it in the mud where it belonged. I took deep, slow breaths and continued fuming into the gray wet day, until I heard a hesitant voice from a little ways down a side-trail.

"Hello?"

I turned.

"Oh, hi," said an old man, hurrying to come near. "I—I don't mean to hold you up. Just… Is this the trail? I mean the Appalachian Trail. In all this rain, I must have missed a marker. Have I made it?"

With an effort, I pulled myself from the deepest depths of my gray mood that matched the weather and forced a smile. "You have made it."

"Oh…great," he said, and hesitantly extended his hand. "Huff 'n puff."

"Huff n' puff?" I hadn't thought either of us was winded enough for such an observation.

"My trail name. I've been chipping away at the trail for years," he said with a chuckle. "I come once a year for a week and walk a section, my wife and me."

I looked around for his wife and wondered how anyone, especially one of an advanced age as Huff 'n Puff, would let their hiking partner out of sight.

"Oh, she's not hiking," he said with a waive. "No no, she drops me off and reads her books and shops for antiques while I'm out here huffing and puffing."

"You don't seem out of breath to me," I said, my smile beginning to feel a tinge more genuine.

"Not nearly so much anymore," he said. "Not since the heart attack."

"Oh!"

He waved away my concern. "Was the best thing that could have happened. Changed my life. Anyway, apparently for a long time, I was hiking with only about one and a half functioning ventricles. I couldn't go more than a hundred steps or so without stopping to catch my breath. Got better as I went along, but… It's a wonder I made it off the trail."

"Huff 'n Puff," I said.

"Huff 'n Puff," he returned with a nod. "Now I'm free from all that. Old and stiff and arthritic, but my heart is strong, and as long as I'm alive, I'll keep coming out here walking these trails. Maybe I'll die out here. I don't know. I don't think that would be too bad a thing."

I didn't know what to say. I didn't have any plans of dying on the Appalachian Trail. I just smiled and shook my head.

"Well, I suppose I should be on my way," he said after a pause ensued. "Just remember, if old Huff 'n Puff can do it, you'll be fine." And with that, he disappeared into the rain heading in the direction I had just come from.

As I walked away, I was truly impressed with the man I had just met, not by outward appearance, but to keep hiking the Appalachian Trail in his previous condition and to still be doing it now... And he wasn't even wearing a rain jacket in all this wet! I had barely met him and just like that, he was gone. I felt connected to him, nonetheless, and was proud of him.

It then occurred to me I was something of a minority on the trail. Most people I came across were either fresh out of high school or college, trying to figure out what to do with their lives before they went on to the "real world", or they were my parents' age or older, their lives drifting away from "that world" into their waning years.

I was 32, in the prime "earning years" of my life, that time when I was supposed to be building my career, raising children, buying a larger home to fit all those kids into, and putting as much money back into a 401K as I could manage. But here I was, divorced, no kids, my home sold, and all the money I had in a checking account. What did that say about me, that I had thrown all that away in one great heave? Was I a broken thing, unfit to handle the world as it was? And what about Huff n' Puff? Was his life over? Was he just riding it out now, the important parts of his journey done? He seemed as happy as anyone I'd ever met. Wasn't that the goal? I didn't feel broken. I felt as whole as I could remember feeling. And yet, I still wanted those things. As much as I valued being out on the trail, I knew I didn't want to spend the rest of my life on the trail trying to figure it out. But what then was I supposed to do? What could I lose myself in so completely? I wanted children. That thought shocked me as I walked. It wasn't that I hadn't wanted them with my wife, I just couldn't see having them in the life we had built. I still wanted financial stability, but with an occupation to call my own, to feel like I was contributing to this world and creating a legacy of that contribution. Ten years into my former life, no matter how much I had "gained," it had never felt like enough.

In some ways, the rushed path from childhood headlong into the "American dream" had left that dream hollow for me, yet here on the trail, I came to believe that it was never really that dream that had failed me but rather, I had failed it…or maybe we had failed each other. I hadn't come to that world of adulthood with the right intentions—purpose over prosperity, value over quantity, meaning over means. I had wanted to gain the world, not realizing I already had it, lived in it, was a part of it, and it was a part of me. And all I needed was to contribute in a way I loved, in a way I wanted.

As I continued walking through the shallow river that had once been the path of the Appalachian Trail, I still didn't know how I wanted to contribute to the world, only that I did and would. I thought, maybe that's what this whole "living" thing was about. I would eventually leave this trail and find what I was going to do in life. I didn't know what that was just yet, and that was okay. As long as I kept putting one foot in front of the other and kept moving forward, I would discover and learn things about myself and others. I was reminded of a quote from one of my favorite philosophers, Alan Watts. "No valid plans for the future can be made by those who have no capacity for living now."

Wherever life took me, I just had to keep moving through it, spending each moment not worrying about what was ahead or behind. I imagined Huff n' Puff smiling as he turned to trudge away from me earlier that day, and I thought about his wife somewhere cozy, reading a book or sifting through bins and aisles in an antique shop, waiting to pick him up again. I smiled. Whatever were the takeaways in life, they seemed to have them figured out. And knowing that made the fact that I was still figuring it out for myself just a little easier.

# 7

## CAN'T TURN OFF THE RAIN

I stopped walking and looked down at my feet, hidden up to my ankles in murky flowing water. Large fat droplets pelted the hood of my rain jacket, so that every time I began to form a coherent calming thought, it was dashed by another set of a thousand echoing splashes. Heavy breaths fumed out of me, and my heart beat like thunder in my chest, though I was not tired, and my ventricles were functioning just fine. I let out a final forced exhale through my nose, looked up into the sky, and shouted, "Just f-cking stop!" then added, "Please!" as though the sky was someone with feelings I should consider.

I cried a little then, just a few tears squeezed out by immense frustration. Then I broke into laughter, the kind I had seen in movies, not in real life. Books describe it as maniacal or unhinged, words that meant the person laughing had lost some part of their attachment to the reality of the present moment. The truth was… I was just extremely frustrated.

The rain had started as just a tiny annoyance… at first. You steel yourself against it without much effort. It's a part of the trail. The ground is still hard and easy to navigate, and your body hasn't lost any warmth yet. A second day of rain isn't much different, a bit of a letdown when you open your eyes to it, but the path is still fine, and there is something to be said about sweating less, even at the cost of some focus and ability to gaze easily around without having to peer past the sides of your rain hood. By the time you reach a fourth day of solid downpour, you begin to wonder what you've done to deserve it. The ground no longer resembles a path. Those who came before you have tromped it into muck, and every step is a labor. You're shivering, even if the weather isn't cold, because every breath of breeze turns your skin into an air conditioner.

The fourth day of rain had come and gone… three days earlier, and I was heading toward the midpoint of a seventh straight day of downpour. In that moment, I couldn't have remembered what happened in the first six if I had focused on only that task. I couldn't remember my thoughts clearly or the face of Huff 'n Puff or where I had stayed or where I was heading. I could have been in Georgia or Maine, and I might have been on a week vacation away from my career and not between that career and the rest of my unknown life. I couldn't see or recall anything through the numbing, blurring effect of non-stop rain.

The trail had become a moving swamp, and I was both Atreyu and his horse, Artax, from *The NeverEnding Story*, wrapped into one person. I was both the puller at the reins and the stubborn beast stamping and throwing back his head, sinking further into despair. But these were not the Swamps of Sadness. These were the Fens of Frustration.

Somewhere in the middle of my mania-induced delirium, I must have taken off my rain jacket. There is something like a memory of me doing it, but it plays out more like one of those movie moments when the character is waking up and isn't sure whether it was a dream or real. I only remember feeling the cold rain soaking my skin through my shirt and facing up into it with my eyes closed. Then I opened them, and something strange happened. When I looked back down at the bog, it didn't look quite so boggish. I could see the edges of the path, water running over in several places to form impromptu rivulets which would eventually join with creeks and rivers further down…but the path was still there, visible.

With a suction, I picked up a foot and let it fall back down a few feet ahead of me and did the same with the other. I repeated this motion until I had moved ten or so feet forward and found I was standing on a bit of harder ground, probably a stretch of bedrock or an old patch of asphalt the path navigated over. I stepped again, and the path was still solid. Another step, and another… slosh, slurp, squish… I stepped along until the ground became soft again.

I stopped and thought about whether I should put my rain jacket back on, then realized I had just had a thought, a clear, whole thought without having to restart it a hundred times due to the thudding of giant raindrops. The drops were still coming, but they were no longer playing the hood of my jacket like a percussion instrument, they were more like a massage on my head, not distracting but rather accentuating my attention to myself and surroundings.

I trudged on with my jacket hanging off the side of my pack and found myself thinking about the last seven days of rain, remembering the places and things done, that I'd met someone named Huff 'n Puff who had a wife, and more than anything else, I had hiked over one hundred miles in that stretch, over one hundred miles during one rain. That more than anything came as a shock to me. Even in my darkest moments of frustration, I had managed to keep putting one foot before the other in succession. For one hundred miles, I had continued making progress, the kind of real progress that would eventually lead me out of the rain.

Though the trail continued to climb and dive, I managed to finish the rest of that day evenly, no deep downs or lofty ups, just calm and present. Sometime after I stopped worrying about the rain, it had stopped falling. I didn't know how long it took after I removed my jacket, it might have been the next mile or the next day, and in that lack of knowledge came a sharp clarity—I realized that was how problems worked. When you quit worrying about them, they ceased being problems.

The next several days were as up and down as the trail itself, mostly up...and up...and up. The Roan Highlands mark a transition between the more rugged and rocky Smokies and the gentler ridges and weathered peaks of the lower Blue Ridge Mountains of North Carolina. Stretching between the Pisgah and Cherokee National Forests, the Roan Highlands rewarded my efforts with scenic grassy balds, offering unhindered views of endless mountain chains stretching into the distance in every direction.

After a few weeks of crisscrossing back and forth between the Tennessee and North Carolina state lines, I followed the trail out of North Carolina for good and enjoyed one last long stretch of miles in the Iron and Holston Mountains of Tennessee before crossing into my fourth state, Virginia. I celebrated the four-hundred-mile mark.

On the day of my fourth century-mile crossing and celebration, the trail gave me another opportunity to pause and
reflect, one unlike anything I'd expected. When setting out
each day, you know you are likely to have your breath stolen a
few dozen times by the myriad natural beauties of the trail—a
hawk swooping low across the trail, a vista down into a gentle
valley—but sometimes it's the experiences that come out of
nowhere that stick clearest in your mind at the end of the day.
The stretch of trail I was walking wasn't peculiar in any way,
the kind of beauty I had experienced for days, peaceful and
relaxing. Then I saw a patch of verdant green up ahead and
stopped at the side of the trail to look at it. It was a patch of
moss growing on the side of the trail in the distinct shape of a
heart. Well-rooted there, it looked like it had grown in exactly
that shape. Had I not been experiencing the world at a walking pace, I never would have noticed it. I felt my chest swell
with something I can only describe as a mix of feeling loved
and seen. I don't know who or what had prepared that moment
for me, but I will never forget it. I continue to carry that with
me today, knowing that it's only when we slow down that we
notice all the beauty surrounding us.

I became sick again shortly after, not as bad as before and
not simply due to dehydration. This was in my stomach, and it
was a continual distraction, discomfort, and discouragement.
Being out on the trail and thus, having no access to such conve-
niences as minute clinics or my local primary care physician,
I focused on drinking lots of water, eating in spread-out small
quantities, and hoping for the best. I continued hiking. At my
sickest point of about a three-day ailment, the day I crossed
into Virginia and to the town I had been looking forward to for

fifty or so miles, I managed to propel myself to what felt like a herculean 10.4 miles, my shortest effort in about a week. I had made it to the town of Damascus, and that alone made me feel somewhat better.

It helped knowing Damascus was my next zero day, and I couldn't help but think just how well-timed that was, almost like a piece of trail magic in itself. My first experience coming into Damascus was the AT logo laid into the bricks of the sidewalks. I couldn't think of a way a town could better say to me, "Hiker's welcome." My second experience was food. I went directly to Mojo's Trailside Café, where I enjoyed a cinnamon bun and a quesadilla in that order. I was so impressed by the quesadilla that I returned two more times during my stay, each time to eat another quesadilla and each time as a snack *between* meals.

I occupied my time in Damascus by walking to the nearby Dollar General for snacks. I also attempted to purchase a book to bring out on the trail and read in the evenings but found only muscled chests and slim babes on the covers and titles, like "Silk is for Seduction" and "Wild Whispers," and opted to leave empty-handed. I made one trip to a rather far-away grocery store to resupply.

Lying in my bed at the Hiker's Inn, I thought about the journey so far, especially the last few days. I thought about the seven straight days of rain and ultimately walking through the last of it jacketless and how so often we tend to protect ourselves from unharmful things. Staring at the ceiling, I chuckled and said to myself, "You can't turn off the rain."

The following realization was the kind that immediately felt like the guidance of an unseen benevolent spirit. Perhaps it was just the offspring of being completely alone, moving at a pace and in a place that allowed for reflection. Maybe that's how all the best insights are born. But from that moment onward, my relationship with the rain changed. I embraced it, accepting it for what it was without frustration. If it was warm enough, I walked without my jacket. If it was cold, I listened to the free percussion performance on my hood.

I thought about how my relationship with the rain related to so many other uncontrollables on the trail and in life. That night, I scribbled in my journal, trying to capture the impact of that lesson. I wrote that life was much like the trail, full of ups and downs, and when I learned to just let go of the problems, they suddenly felt so much smaller. Michael A. Singer put it best, I think, when he said, "The truth is that most of life will unfold in accordance with forces far outside your control, regardless of what your mind says about it."

If I couldn't turn off the rain, I might as well make the best of it.

# 8

## MISCHIEF AND MAYHEM

Coming down over a drop, the trail bent to the left, and I stopped suddenly, every hair on my body set instantly on end.

"What is that?" I said aloud, even though I knew exactly what I was looking at. There was nothing else in the world which could strike such a distinct and imposing figure in the mind of a thru-hiker. What confused me was not the identity of the creature itself. I was in a state of shock at seeing one so large, so close, so directly in front of me, and me so alone.

The bear was large, larger than you realize bears are, even when you know how large they can get because you've read about them extensively in thru-hiking guidebooks. Whatever you have in your mind, when there is one in front of you, suddenly it is twice that big. This one was a dark chocolate brown with a milk chocolate muzzle and looked like it had been eating well since waking up from its sleep a few months before. It sat just off the trail about twenty feet this side of the next white blaze and about the same distance from me.

"Hey b-b-b—," I stuttered. His nose flared. I cleared my throat. "Hey bear," I began again, speaking from deep within my chest, trying to sound calm but confident, attempting to match all the instructions in the guides I'd read to prepare for this unlikely moment.

The bear didn't move. He—I don't know why I think it was a he, but that's what I thought, so that's what I will write—*he* just looked at me. There was so much intelligence in his eyes, and I don't know if that made the moment scarier or less scary. It was as if, while I was contemplating my next move, he was trying to decide whether I was worth bothering with. He sniffed and licked the air and shifted in his seat, and I shifted in my boots, taking a step backward. I scanned the area and saw a large boulder just off the trail near me. Growing up in rural and well-wooded northern New Jersey, I knew the best thing I could do was to make myself look as large as possible.

I scrambled onto the boulder and quickly turned to face the bear again, hoping he'd be gone but half expecting to see him barreling toward me. But there he was, still sitting and staring at me like I was a show he was going to watch to the end.

"Hey bear!" I shouted and raised my trekking pole above my head horizontally so that it made a triangle with my two arms. "Hey bear, hey bear, hey bear!"

The bear stood suddenly, and my mind raced wondering what I had just set in motion. Had making myself "large" done the trick? Or had I just become dinner after the show? The bear extended up to its full height, nearly as tall as me even though I was elevated above the ground on top of a large boulder. Then he slammed the dirt in front of him with both massive paws like the ground was a nut he was trying to crack open, and I feared it actually might. I felt the boulder tremble slightly beneath me.

That wasn't in the guide, I thought. What *had* been in the guide, I remembered painfully in that moment, was the recommendation that if I was hiking the Appalachian Trail during the spring, summer, or fall, I should carry both a portable foghorn and a can of bear spray. I had neither, both falling victim to my confidence that there hadn't been a bear attack on the AT in several years and that one was so incredibly unlikely that I shouldn't bother with the added weight. I felt the absence of those survival tools like phantom pain in an amputated limb.

I knew, viscerally, standing there on a boulder nearly five hundred miles into the wilderness that this was one of those moments, the ones where the decision you make next could either end your hike or end something much more important.

*Added weight!* I thought and would have thrown everything else out of my pack in that instant to have the added weight of bear spray.

"Hey bear!" I tried one last time, and the bear stomped again. I knew this creature was trying to give a specific response to my call. It felt almost playful or, at the very least, curious. If I hadn't been absolutely terrified and rightly concerned about being eaten alive, I might have tossed a stick in the air toward it, just to see what he would do. Fetch or murder? It could even be both, I thought with a brief, morbid chuckle.

I threw no sticks. It was clear we were at an impasse, and I was either going to have to double back and wait to hike this section again with more boots causing noise on the trail or make as wide of a path around the giant mammal as I could and hope for the best.

"Hey bear," I said much more softly as I crept off the boulder and came to stand again on the gravel. "Heeeey bear," I said again slowly, and took a first step, more to soothe myself, I think, than to have any effect on this massive animal. I stepped off the path and drew an arc with my line of vision, one that I would follow through the woods, back to the path, whose center point was a 400-pound carnivore. I took a first step onto that invisible arc...*crunch*...pause, then another, and froze as the bear huffed. I stayed still for some amount of time that my then terrified state could not allow me to properly recall. Keeping my eyes on the imaginary arc, I stepped again... and again, around a tree trunk and a few shrubs, then back onto the semicircle. I kept stepping and stepping, crunching leaves and twigs, and with every step, I trained my eyes on the arc, shutting out thoughts that the crunching my boots made was actually the crunching of massive paws. Finally, I realized I had stepped back onto the trail at the same location as the next white blaze, with the bear, once again, about twenty feet away, only this time behind me. I glanced toward it for the first time since stepping off the trail. The bear had come back to sitting, now facing north toward me. I stepped backward once...twice...a third time, then turned away. I walked away with an even, slow pace, my heart beating like I had just sprinted all the way from Damascus.

The rest of that day, while no less eventful, was decidedly and delightfully less death-defying. Not long after the encounter with the bear, I took as planned the most difficult side-trail of the entire hike. Many thru-hiking purists, like myself, are split on their views of side trails in general. To be a purist in its simplest definition means to hike the entire distance of the trail without any aid from machinery or others carrying your pack, to walk past every single white blaze under your own weight.

To make sure I was adhering to thru-hike purism, whenever I hitchhiked into town at the intersection of the trail and a local roadway, when I made it back to the trail, each time, I made sure to cross to the side of the road I had hiked from, touch the edge of the pavement with my hand, and then continue across the road onto the next white blaze. Side-trails are not argued to in any way jeopardize this; they are simply seen as distractions—unnecessary, tiring, resource-intensive distractions. I never had a single thought of doubt about whether or not I would hike the Mt. Rogers Side Trail. To worry about such things, I thought to myself as I rounded onto the detour, would be to hike someone else's hike, and I had stopped doing that the moment I left my career.

Mt. Rogers is the highest natural point in Virginia. I arrived at the very top of its 5,729-foot crown and looked out, confused. There was no view at all. The entire peak was surrounded by thick forest. Disappointed, I found the survey marker indicating the summit and took a seat. I imagined what the views might look like if the summit were above the tree line. Something amazing happened. I wasn't disappointed anymore. I had accepted the problem and moved on in the best way I could. I began to appreciate the fact that this highest point in Virginia didn't have a view, a lesson about expectations and maybe a metaphor about some efforts being only about the effort itself and not some tangible reward at the end.

There was something symbolic about not only being on this several-months-long adventure but also making the decision to extend it by a few miles and several thousand feet of elevation, only to arrive with nothing but my thoughts and imagination at what was beyond. I wasn't focused on "getting to the end" so I could get back home and figure out my life. I was enjoying the adventure, seeking it out, and accepting all that came with it. I had given myself permission to wander and to experience all the wondrous and awe-inspiring surprises life would place in my path as I did. There were no wild roses on top of Mt. Rogers, but if there had been, I would have stopped and given them a sniff.

While I didn't see any wild roses in the Grayson Highlands, wild is exactly how the state website describes the ponies that live there. That is not what I would call them. Perhaps once, many decades or even centuries ago, when man had not yet carved its dominion out of this area of the world, they were. But now, these creatures' health is being cared for by state employees and they are being passed, petted, and fed by many thousands of visitors and hikers each year, the ponies of Grayson Highlands are no longer wild. In fact, they are as close to tame, if not tamer than any horse, pony, mule, or donkey I have ever seen. I would, however, describe them as mischievous.

I came upon a small herd as I crossed over one of the many balds in the highlands, just where the guides said they were most likely to be found. They were grazing along the trail, so I stopped and as so many hikers have done in the past, I stabbed my trekking poles into the soft ground, flipped my phone into selfie mode, and positioned for a photo, just me and the pony. The pony lifted his head and seemed perfectly happy to have his picture taken, like it had rehearsed the moment. But this pony had a friend.

Before I could finish positioning my camera, one of my trekking poles began trekking its own way down the trail without me…in the mouth of a pony. Apparently, this is a known thing, one of the many things I didn't know until the reality was forced upon me. Ponies, as I now understand, love salt, and after more than 500 miles of depositing layer upon layer of sweat into the handles of my trekking poles, they were turned into an equine delicacy.

Mischievous the ponies of Grayson Highlands are, and also playful. This one seemed more interested in taking me for a quick jaunt through the tufts and hillocks of the bald than he did keeping my trekking pole or eating the handle. By the end, I was certain he had done this exact thing before and knew he wasn't getting a quick snack but rather just wanted to play. After a couple minutes, he slowed and allowed me to catch up. I reached for the pole, and he released it willingly, and then, as if to say, "I was only kidding around," he stood patiently while I took a selfie with him, one of my favorite pictures from the trail.

A few miles later, I celebrated the five-hundred-mile mark by making my usual "500" rock structure homage. Shortly after, I ran into BAMF again, and once more, he was living up to the enjoyable irony of his trail name. I approached Wise Shelter at about 3:00 in the afternoon, and there he was, sleeping.

# 9

## A STAYING GLOW

I had an inauspicious approach to the quarter-way mark of the trail. Late in the day, rain had begun to fall suddenly and hard. Much like roads tend to be slick when the raindrops first hit them, and before there is enough accumulation to wash away the grime, so also are roots as I came to learn. I was walking along, unconcerned, as the trail was still nice and firm when the arch of my trail runners found a slippery root and sent me in a sort of sideways karate kick. I ate it hard. As I sat there in the dirt being rained on, I told myself two things. The first was that I had made it five hundred miles without falling, not a small feat. And the second—it was already time for new shoes.

I had only hiked one quarter of the total distance of the trail. I had gone through two pairs of hiking shoes, the first pair retired early from their role in this adventure before they could permanently damage me, the second I was still wearing as I crossed the quarter-way mark, well beyond their expected life, and to whom I would soon be bidding farewell at the Woods Hole Hostel, where a new pair awaited me. Thirty-six days and nights had come and gone, thirty-six sunrises and sunsets, many of which I had enjoyed a front-row seat to, and a few pairs of which I even experienced from the same location. I had visited many towns, ascended and descended tens of thousands of feet of elevation, seen a host of animals I had never seen before in my life, several of which I didn't think I would be lucky enough to glimpse. And most shockingly, I had traveled over 500 miles. It felt like I had lived an entire life of a sort on the trail, one distinctly different from the one that preceded and one I knew would be equally different from the one that would follow. And yet, I needed to live that lifespan, or one like it, three more times before I would reach the summit of Mt. Katahdin.

The first leg of that day had brought me to Atkins, Virginia, where a very hiker-popular Mexican food restaurant sat attached to an Exxon Mobil gas station. It's hard to objectively judge how good food really is when you eat it on the trail. On the one hand, my memory of food experiences from the hike are almost universally that what I ate on the trail was the best food I ever had. That is not an exaggeration. Almost every time I ate, I thought I was eating some pure, perfect version of a meal I'd had throughout my life. On the other hand, I have never been hungrier at any point than during those grueling miles. I worry that if I ever returned to some of these places, I might learn that they were in fact just serving the kind of food you might expect from a Mexican food restaurant attached to a gas station. Regardless, those were some of the best fajitas I can remember, and I choose to leave that memory the way it is.

After lunch, I continued until I reached the trail crossing with Virginia State Highway 610. From there, I left the trail and trekked a short distance along a very quiet back road to the Quarter Way Inn, a hostel run by past thru-hikers, where I would enjoy a warm shower and a comfortable bed, the first of either since Damascus.

The next morning, I used my night of rest to fuel a new record stretch in a single day, 24.7 miles. It felt longer, maybe because of the enjoyment of the relative ease of meal access the previous few days. I had done a poor job of calorie management and never stopped to eat during the day, throwing back a few bites of this and that as I walked, never giving my body enough of a break at any point to feel rested. That, no doubt, played a part...though I think the scenery was the more likely culprit.

I want to make sure you understand that Virginia was absolutely beautiful, stunning, everything people said it would be and more...so it's hard for me to say what I'm going to say next. There is another reality to hiking for any long stretch of days in Virginia—and that is, Virginia can be a long difficult slog of monotony. There is even a name for it—the "Virginia blues". In between the spread-out vistas and soul-cleansing waterfalls, beyond the few balds and knobs in the southwestern portion of the state, you enter it one day, not knowing you have. The woods seem to invite you into an enchanting experience, like stepping through the looking glass into a shaded, misty green world...then you never come back out again. After losing track of time and space, you realize you have no idea how long or far you've been trekking through this green wormhole. It's beautiful, yes. But every day feels like you are passing the same trunks, the same treed slopes, the same trickle and whisper of water. And this goes on for 556 miles, the longest stretch of the Appalachian Trail in any state.

I felt it that day hiking from VA 610 almost twenty-five miles to Jenkins Shelter…and over twenty-three miles the following day to Jenny Knob Shelter, passing the 600-mile mark along the way. Shortly after, something penetrated the "Virginia blues".

It was early in the morning when I came upon my first encounter with an experience I had read about but never witnessed. The clouds parted, and the trees were situated in such a way that the beams of light coming through the cracks felt like you could reach out and scoop a piece of the golden light into your hands. Later, as I studied to become a nature therapist, I learned that the Japanese have a word for this—Komorebi. It means "sunlight coming through the trees". It was so surreal, I paused to take it in, to not let the moment slip by. I closed my eyes and lifted my face to the sun's rays and felt energy move through me, like a young sapling vying for warmth beneath the shade of its elders. It's hard to put words to the feeling I had in that place. I'm not sure I knew what enlightenment feels like, but I imagine it being something like that experience. In my life today, I seek out moments like this, like a nature scavenger hunter. When I catch them, I'm reminded that I'm exactly where I need to be at exactly the right time.

I stood for a few minutes thinking how I might never have seen that if I hadn't taken this chance, this leap of faith into the unknown, of leaving the career for mountain hiking, and how so many people would never see this in their lifetime, trapped behind their computer and phone screens. I carried a gratefulness with me as I continued through the slightly less predictable miles of Virginia.

On my climb towards Woods Hole Hostel, my spirits were lightened a bit more, not just at the thought of reaching my third set of trail runners and all the relief my feet would soon be feeling. But I also had an unexpected encounter on the trail with what I believed was a pile of someone's discarded equipment. I saw the mound of stuff near the top of a rise, just at the edge of the path, and began contemplating what might lead someone to discard so much and why not at any of the shelters or hostels before or after. Was there some danger? Were they forced to jettison their pack and run away? Had they experienced a psychotic break? That was not unheard of out here.

The answer became apparent as I neared. This wasn't a pile of discarded things at all. It was a whole pile of person, things attached. My mind went in a very different direction, wondering if this person was injured, and what I would do if he was so deep in the woods. As I approached slowly, the man startled and clambered to his feet, arms and equipment all akimbo as though I had jumped out of the bushes. I was both shocked and relieved, even though he was incredibly gaunt and equally dirty, even by trail standards.

"What time is it?" he asked frantically. "Nevermind, I'm late anyway!"

"Late?" I asked.

He shushed me. In the span of about the next fifteen seconds, he explained that his trail name was Knots, pointing to his full head of dreads, and that he was late because when you're doing what he was doing, you were always late. What he was, in fact, doing was attempting to break the self-supported speed record for the Appalachian Trail of 54 days and seven hours. He had to go right now. And go he did.

"What day are you on now?" I shouted after him as he sped away looking like a sprinting skeleton.

"Twelve!"

*That's right, Ryan, twelve…* I thought. I needed a little time to let that settle in. Here I was on my thirty-eighth day, and this guy, who looked like he was just as likely to fall asleep and never wake up again as he was to finish the trail at all, had traveled the same 600-plus miles I had *in less than two weeks*! For a moment, I was disheartened. He would be done in maybe forty or so more days, a little over a month. By my best guess, I had over three times that left. I took a breath and remembered that I wasn't here to "finish" the Appalachian Trail. I was here to "hike" it. Finishing was just something I hoped to do at the end.

I was more than a little surprised to run into Knots later that day at a small deli along the trail in Bland, VA. Apparently, even when you're trying to break the speed record for the AT, you still have to stop and eat. While there, a truck pulled up, and a man got out and walked into the deli, gave us a look-over and scoffed, then continued to the counter. While ordering, he looked back at us no less than twice, each time looking more disgusted than the previous.

"Hikers, huh?" he said with a dismissive tone as he took a seat a few tables away.

"Yup," I said. "Hoping to hike the whole AT."

"I figured," he said and buried his head into a few bites. "Why aren't you working?"

"Working?"

"Yeah, working. You know, when you do a task and get paid for it."

I glanced at Knots, who was doing a better job than me of finding the situation amusing.

"That's what's wrong with the world," the man continued. "Your whole generation, you think you can just hike trolly-la through life. Someone else'll just take care of everything for you. That ain't how it works, son. You and your silent friend there, you should be working hard, learning what it means to be a man, not going on some damned camping adventure."

"Actually—" I began to launch an ill-advised counter to everything I'd just heard.

"No, I don't want to hear it," said the man, cutting me off. "Not a word of it." The man stood and began toward the door. "Work," he said, launching his final grenade before letting the door shut behind him.

There was a short silence at our table broken by Knots. "Well, guess he's going back to work…"

Then Knots and I both broke out laughing. He had summed up the exchange well.

The next day, I met two people who were as close to the opposite of the "working" man at the deli as I can imagine. Woods Hole Hostel is one of the oldest and frankly, most amazing hostels on the trail. It's run by two people who never thru-hiked the trail, Mike and Neville, but as I learned the night I stayed there, they carry on building upon a legacy much older than themselves. Mike was a very nice and polite guy but also, I gathered—in the no-more-than-five minutes he spent among the hikers—a bit of an introvert, leaving Neville by both design and nature to play the role of host, server, and historian. She was in general just an all-around amazing person, of which I can't imagine anyone doing a finer job. Though I could never confirm this, I assume that means Mike spends most of his time doing the behind-the-scenes tasks related to food production, and a lot of tasks that would be, indeed. One of the most impressive things about the Woods Hole hostel is the fact that every bit of food you eat there is made from ingredients that are raised or grown at Woods Hole Hostel. The bread, the cheese, even the ice cream—all of it comes from their small farm and garden practice.

After settling in, I showered and wandered their amazing property, taking advantage of an afternoon of resting. That evening, thoroughly stuffed with what is perhaps *truly* the finest fare I had ever eaten, I sat with my feet soaking in a salt bath beside a fire while Neville held a group of about twenty thru-hikers in rapt attention as she gave a complete history of the Woods Hole Hostel and her grandfather, the man who had started it. Much more than the details of the story, I remember just how much Neville glowed while telling it. It was a familiar glow, not one of an old friend but rather a new acquaintance, the kind of meeting you instantly know will always play a special part in your life; it was the glow that comes from doing exactly what you wanted to be doing more than anything else and having absolutely no doubts about it, the one I had felt over the last thirty-nine days.

I lay in bed that night thinking about this glow, wondering and worrying a little if I would lose it once I was off the trail, whether I would be able to find exactly what I wanted to be doing more than anything else back in "the real world". I carried those thoughts with me as I left the next morning, and I'm not sure they left me for the rest of the trail, not fully. I'd had dreams of beginning a company focused on outdoor adventures even before venturing out onto the AT and certainly since, living a life of simplicity in a van or an RV and traveling around the country. Both of those sounded like a lot of fun, but could I make money doing that? Could I support myself? A wife? Children? Could I have this glow I felt now…and a life? Or was the truth of it that this was just a lone adventure, a phase between the old version of me and the next one I'd become, once the realities of life kicked in once again?

These thoughts combined, no doubt, with the Virginia blues and had me feeling everything and wondering about everything as I continued my trek along the blue ridges and the even bluer valleys of Virginia. BAMF and Woodpecker—who I had just met a few days before—were with me most of that thoughtful and wondering stretch. There was always a child-like enthusiasm and free-spiritedness about Woodpecker that kept me from slipping too deep into contemplation. To tell the truth, I wanted to relate these thoughts out loud, but there was something that kept stopping me, like I didn't want to rain on anyone else's hike with the somberness I was drifting in and out of. And maybe I didn't want to say them out loud, as though hearing them in my own voice or spoken back to me in someone else's would make them realer than they were trapped inside my head.

The night after Woods Hole Hostel, BAMF and Wood-pecker were sitting on a ridge at our campsite, enjoying the incredible vista toward Peterstown, West Virginia, when BAMF asked, "Hey Scrambler, do you want some sleepy-time tea?"

Woodpecker and I looked at each other and chuckled, as though we had both been in on an inside joke that stretched back years. Something about the thought of this larger-than-life guy, who went by the name BAMF, asking something so domestic, so refined… yet childlike, had us in stitches. As it happened, the offer might have been better called "meaningful-time" tea. That night, as we looked out to the deepening purple vista that stretched into West Virginia and watched the brightening moon and stars, we talked about everything that was on our minds—what came before the trail, why we were here, what we thought might come after, our biggest fears, our deepest thoughts, and our wildest dreams. I learned that BAMF was missing his girl back home. They were just at that point in the relationship where things might get serious soon, and he was excited to see what the future held for them. Woodpecker was fresh out of college. She was using the trail as a buffer before settling into a career. She didn't know exactly what that career would be yet and was a little nervous about it.

I admired Woodpecker so much for that choice, one that many likely had tried talking her out of. I wondered what I might have learned about myself had I given myself the freedom, when I was fresh out of college, the permission to wander and contemplate what I wanted from my life. When I'm counseling young people now and asked if they should do something similar, I always and wholeheartedly recommend that they do, if they have the chance.

When it was my turn to say what I was going to do next, after I summited Katahdin or left the trail before it, I surprised myself by saying with complete belief, "I don't know what I'll do, but whatever it is, I'm going to do it honestly. I'm going to help people, and I'm going to find a way to show them all this."

# 10

## DETOUR FOR THE SOUL

The "Virginia blues" seemed a little less blue the next few days as BAMF, Woodpecker, and I continued on together from that beautiful ridgeline near Rice Field Shelter. The weather hadn't changed, and the broadleaves and pine needles hadn't suddenly shifted in their hues. Rather, a lens was removed, one I hadn't known had been tinting my view. By opening up to my travel mates the night before, I had released a fear of the unknown future beyond the trail and replaced it with excitement for the same. I stopped ruminating about what could go wrong and gazed toward the future with the same wonderment I felt toward the great vistas of the trail. What lay beyond the deep green forests at trail's end was filled with endless possibilities. I didn't know what was in store yet, but like friends I had yet to meet, I eagerly and joyfully wondered about them and how different and unique those experiences were going to be.

A few southbounders approached one morning, and when we reached a polite engaging distance, we gave each other the perfunctory nods that meant we wanted to be polite but not necessarily start up a conversation. In passing, I noticed one of their faces twist curiously at me. He slowed and turned, looking at me as he walked away backward. "You sure have a big ol' smile on your face."

"Beautiful weather and a brand-new pair of kicks," I replied, and they said something like "right on" as they continued south.

I chuckled to myself at just how free my response had been, like it had come from someone else entirely. I had come from a world of overthinking and polishing anything I said, but this had blurted out with no hesitation. I was comfortable in my own skin, in my own thoughts and present actions, in a way I could only remember from those innocent childhood years.

I carried that unbounded joyfulness into my longest day yet, more than twenty-five miles, followed by what became one of the most spontaneous days of the entire trip. It was our plan to hike about 18 miles that day, leaving us just shy of the 700-mile mark and the first of three stopping points on the heralded Virginia Triple Crown—Dragon's Tooth, which was followed by McAfee Knob, then Tinker Cliffs. Route 42 intersected the trail about eight miles into the morning at a place that felt exactly in the middle of a place called nowhere. No sounds of vehicles and no sign except for the blacktop roadway signaled that civilization existed here. But some invisible force must have communicated between our stomachs as we stood on the side of the road with a choice to cross and keep hiking. We all suddenly looked at each other and spontaneously blurted out, "…Burger?"

We each laughed at our shared mindset and agreed that a trip into whatever town we were nearest was just the impromptu adventure we had all come out on the trail to have.

There was something energizing about breaking from the established plans to enjoy the freedom one had on the trail. After about thirty minutes of waiting, a car slowed next to us. It was an older vehicle, maybe an Oldsmobile, with a look that might have made me a little uneasy to climb into in my previous life. But this was the new Ryan, who probably looked more worse for wear and far scarier to the person driving this clunker, not to mention the two people beside me looking just as dubious.

"Where you headed?" said a slight woman through a window that either didn't roll down all the way or had been intentionally left only a third of the way cracked.

I looked at BAMF and Woodpecker and without any words, turned back to the cracked window and said, "Cheeseburgers?"

She laughed. "Get in! I'll take you to Blacksburg. That's where I'm heading for work. It's a bit of a drive, but there isn't a decent burger closer in any direction. And sorry about the smell, I think I've got a family of dead mice somewhere in here."

Again, the three of us glanced at each other silently, recognizing that Chelsea and her family of mice were the perfect ride.

Chelsea dropped us off on one end of the main drag through town and suggested, "Just walk into town. You'll find plenty of options." There certainly were. Fortunately, none of us were the type to get paralyzed by an abundance of choices, and we quickly landed on a place called Sharky's. It couldn't have been any better. Not only was it "buy one, get one" burger day, but there was a pool table, a much-needed recreation to break up the green tunnel we'd been staring into for the last several days. I didn't realize until we were seated that I had already eaten there on a road trip as a young kid with my childhood best friend and his dad. It was strange revisiting a place at such a different point in my life, both familiar and different, like those two versions of me were.

After burgers and billiards, we decided there were still more calories to be had and found our way to a frozen yogurt place. The 20.8 ounces my overflowing cup weighed in at was a full five ounces more than the weight of my sleeping bag, and I wondered as I spooned it in just how much that would help or hurt my next few miles.

We were so taken aback by how awesome Blacksburg was and were likely still thinking about how long it had taken us to hitch there in the first place, that we decided to turn the day into a "nearo," a day of relatively few miles, and stay the night—a decision that would have caused my previous hyper-plan-everything-out self to break out in hives. Instead, I was glowing and smiling and basking in the fresh adventure.

We were about ten calls in to our pursuit of accommodations for the night when we began to wonder if we should begin looking for a place behind a dumpster. I started scanning the street for places a sleeping bag would go unnoticed when a man walked up to us outside the yogurt shop, took a sip of his coffee, and said, "Hikers? A friend of mine owns a hotel here in town, just down the road there. Mention my name, Mark. I'm sure he'll give you a room."

I was still reeling from the kindness of the surprise visitor when a car slowed opposite us on the street. "Do you need a ride?"

"Thank you, but we're just going a couple of blocks," I said.

"Thru-hikers?"

We confirmed.

"I'll take ya. I'm Little Bear."

Little Bear, as we learned that evening, had thru-hiked the AT a couple of years prior. Ever since her hike, she had been wanting to pass on all the kindness she'd experienced from the many trail angels she'd encountered. When she saw us sitting on the curb, she was overwhelmed by the desire to help us any way she could. That ended up being several ways. Not only did she let us sleep in her living room for free, she washed our clothes, let us use her shower, and drove us back into town that evening for dinner.

Back at her house later that evening with full bellies, we sat with Little Bear in her living room, and her roommate joined us, along with Patty and Cricket, her two dogs. We chatted about our adventures so far, and she nodded along and smiled and laughed at the similar memories, the same way people who grew up in the same town might enjoy stories at a high school reunion.

When it was her turn to share, we followed along with the same fondness at the places which were so fresh on our hearts. That fondness turned to a kind of awe when she related the story of her final ascent to the top of Katahdin. When she talked about the relief, pride, and joy of being there, and the mix of fears and longing for it to continue but knowing that it couldn't, BAMF, Woodpecker, and I all shared silent tears. It wasn't any particular way she had described it, just the immense amount of space the thought of finishing the AT took up in my being. An evening of stories was all we had shared, but I felt like Little Bear became a part of my family that night, along with the two other thru-hikers sitting with me.

The next morning, Little Bear handed me a cup of coffee in a mug that read "good f—cking morning," and it was. She cooked us eggs and bacon and drove us back to where we had hitched from the day before. From there, we decided we would at the very least finish our planned remaining miles from the previous day.

The first climb came almost immediately after we crossed Route 42. I felt like I had lost some of the stamina I'd gained over the previous six weeks, likely due to the massive amount of Blacksburg sustenance working its way through me. But it wasn't long before I found my legs again and was able to enjoy the beautiful scenery. Several times during the climb, the path would edge a cliffside, offering inspiring views of the nearby valleys and green peaks. Then another presented itself, requiring no cliffside but resting directly in the middle of the trail.

"Trail magic!" said Woodpecker, as we huddled around a peanut butter sandwich.

"Why is the baggy open?" I asked, to which we all decided we had better not trust this bit of trail offering. BAMF picked it up and put it in his pack, and we were all a bit thoughtfully quiet for several steps before the next item appeared, the filter of a spent cigarette. Shortly after, the mystery was solved when we came upon a jar of Smucker's Goober—peanut butter and jelly combined into a single container.

We turned to each other uncomfortably. "Jazz Band," I said, and we walked on in silence.

The night before Blacksburg and the newly coined Little Bear Hostel, BAMF, Woodpecker, and I had stayed at War Spur Shelter with several other hikers. The shelter was full, and preferring to sleep in privacy, I was setting up my tent outside when a scene caught my attention, the kind that took a few minutes to wrap your head around, and the more you did, the less good you felt about it. A man was sitting by himself at a picnic table crying.

"What do you think that's about?" BAMF asked.

"He's been at it all afternoon," a nearby hiker spoke barely above a whisper. "His trail name's Jazz Band, and that's about all anyone has been able to get from him. Doesn't want to talk, doesn't seem to want anything."

Everything from Jazz Band's pack was laid out in front of him the way you might to let them dry out in the breeze, but nothing was wet. And he was just crying. He cried for about five minutes as I set up my tent, then he stopped abruptly like a faucet had been turned off. He began to stare at his hands with an unsettlingly angry look on his face. There were about fifteen cigarette butts scattered among the strewn contents of his pack. He lit another and smoked it, shaking the entire time. When it was gone, he flicked it into the pile and began crying again. I tried to not observe much more than this, not wanting to be caught watching. But that appeared to be his activity the entire evening.

At one point, I offered him a snack. I had certainly done my share of crying on the trail by that point, and I hoped a little human contact would do him some good. He accepted the snack, pulled the wrapper open, then paused. For a moment, I thought it just as likely that he would tear up again for the kind gesture or throw the opened package into the nearby treeline. Instead, he handed it back to me and said, "Actually, no thanks," and pulled another cigarette from his pack.

When the rest of us retired to our beds for the night, he was still sitting at the table, smoking, crying, shaking, a dozen or so more empty filters around him, and no sign of setting up camp. BAMF, Woodpecker, and I slept with our knives within easy reach. The next morning, he was gone, most of his items gone with him. The filters left sitting on the table were the only sign he had been there.

After finding the jar of Goober on the trail, the rest of the items that had been laid out on the table in front of Jazz Band appeared further down the path. Each time we came upon another piece of gear or bit of food, we would stop and look around, half fearing we'd find Jazz Band staring back at us, half fearing we wouldn't. We'd pick up each item and stow them away to be given away or discarded somewhere off the trail, or returned to Jazz Band if we came across him.

The whole situation felt like being witnesses at a crime scene. We all believed Jazz Band must have had some kind of psychotic episode, and his pack items scattered across a mile of trail were the final signals of a break. I was worried worse had happened to him. Afterward, I attempted to look him up. I didn't know his off-trail name and never found anything out. For the purpose of privacy, I've changed his trail name to Jazz Band and hope if he reads this, he will recognize himself in that name.

Jazz Band, if you're out there, I wish I could have done something more for you. I hope you're doing well and that you made it to safety and to help. We all struggle sometimes. We shouldn't have to do it alone.

# 11

## WHO COOKS FOR YOU?

After the last bit of evidence marking the disappearance of Jazz Band was found, we were soon introduced to one of the most spectacular stretches of the Appalachian Trail, the three signature locations of the Virginia Triple Crown: Dragon's Tooth, McAfee Knob, and Tinker Cliffs. We needed the welcome diversion to shift our thoughts back to the trail, and this stretch of well-visited locations lived up to the implied royalty of its name.

When approaching many of the dramatically named locations along the Appalachian Trail, I felt an anticipation mixed with excitement and fear—excitement that I was about to experience something new, where many before me had stood in wonder and where I would contemplate new thoughts unique to me and some no doubt shared by the multitude of past thru-hikers; and fear that the reality wouldn't live up to the anticipation, like places I had encountered previously on the trail that bore names invoking trepidation or awe that left one puzzled and slightly disappointed. Dragon's Tooth had the name and the reputation, and it lived up to them both spectacularly.

Approaching the thirty-five-foot-tall gray spire, I allowed my mind to wander into mythical imaginings. I pictured a giant fantastical beast lying on its back in its final resting place, a single lone but massive tooth remaining after the plundering of weather and time washed all else away.

Standing in its shadow as the sun began to set that night, I felt a reverence, nothing short of what it might have been if that story were true. I tried to imagine, instead of some great dragon, what that peak might have looked like a thousand years ago, a million years, one hundred million, when the climate was different, when there might have been dragons roaming nearby instead of wild ponies. I tried to imagine myself existing that long. What would I have seen and felt in that great passage of time? What would I have survived? Long periods of ice…drought…the death of species…the birth of others.

I pictured myself as a speck along that timeline, just a passerby here to whisper "hello" and then "so long" to this ancient silent watcher of the world. I felt connected to that somehow, and that made me feel so small in the grand scheme of nature and yet so much bigger resting on the perch of that giant history. It seemed almost insignificant marking "700" with small rocks at Dragon's Tooth. But that made it all the more significant to me, knowing that my story was connected in some small way with the mountain's.

You are not allowed to camp at Dragon's Tooth, and I make no claims here that I did…or didn't. And I do not offer any recommendation for whether you should or shouldn't, either. What I will say is that there are few better sunrises than the one offered at this incredible vista.

The day after Dragon's Tooth, we arose early and shook off our hiker hobble with a goal of arriving at McAfee Knob by midday. Roughly twelve miles later, we stepped out onto the 270-degree natural viewing platform, showcasing the Catawba Valley and the many surrounding ridges and saddles. It was one of the first times, despite my self-image of a confident, brave man, that I literally scooted on my behind for fear of tumbling to my death.

McAfee Knob could more accurately be called "McAfee Extremely Unsettling Ledge." It is comprised of a series of what appear like those flat, platelike mushrooms that jut out from the trunk of a tree which form little platforms, seemingly for small elves or sprites. I don't know how far the furthest of these platforms cantilevered out from the face of the knob, but standing there at the edge of McAfee, with the wind gusting around me, I felt like I was a mile into open air, and at any moment, the whole thing was going to come crumbling down around me. It was as terrifying and bewildering as it was amazing and beautiful. And I'm incredibly glad I did it.

After descending McAfee Knob, the sky released its captured precipitation, forcing us to wait before attempting to climb back up the slopes to the third destination of the Triple Crown, Tinker Cliffs. This put us a little behind in our hike for the day, and as we emerged above the trees onto the ledge, we were grateful to find that the sun had not set. Once again, we were treated to nature's canvas of magenta pinks and deepening violet purple above an undulating sea of cornflower blue as the mountain peaks darkened in twilight. As dusk settled on the landscape, the stars began to twinkle more brightly, marking the end of sunset. We rested and watched the entire display, despite knowing we still had a few miles of hiking into the night ahead of us.

We left Tinker Cliffs, headlamps strapped on, making our way in the dark to the closest shelter. During that last stretch, we saw more frogs than I have ever seen in my life, so many I had to watch where I placed every step to avoid squishing the hoppers. They were big and bold, jumping into the path ahead of us, some hopping one or two plops along the trail in front of our feet before diving back into the shrubs and puddles on either side.

After arriving and setting up our tents, huddled in lamplight, the night animals began the singing portion of the evening performance. The frogs were first, of course, perhaps thanking us for not stepping on them. Then came cicadas and crickets to join the chorus behind the night birds' haunting solos. We were discussing the goal for the next day, a stretch that would bring us into a town about ten miles away called Daleville, when a particularly interesting call floated down from right overhead. It was the call of the Barred Owl, the first time I'd heard it on the trail. The call sounded like words being spoken, but I couldn't figure out what they were. Woodpecker must have had the same thoughts. After about three or four rounds from the Barred Owl, she said in a hooty voice, "Who cooks for you? Who cooks for you all?" BAMF and I simultaneously exclaimed in excitement that she was correct, that was exactly what the Barred Owl seemed to be saying.

Out on the trail, one spends a great deal of time dreaming of the next meal or the great one had before. And so, it is entirely possible that the only reason we were so certain of what the Barred Owl was saying was because it lined up perfectly with what our stomachs were thinking. This somewhat comically hooted question would come to factor much more into my life post-trail. Among other ways of showing people the value I experienced on the Appalachian Trail, I now lead nature therapy, commonly called Forest Bathing, in the woods. Part of my program includes this call-and-answer. Usually with a group of fifteen to twenty teens or young adults, I explain the words, then we use the sounds given to me by the Barred Owl. I call out the first part, "Who cooks for you?" after which, the group faces away from me, toward all those who may have wandered too far, and they sound out, "Who cooks for you all?"

It's a simple idea, one with the practical purpose of making sure everyone remains within calling distance of the group, but I often think about people I've known, ones who—like myself for a time—wandered too far, away from the group, apart from genuine connection, separated from self.

I don't know if I would have answered if someone had called to me during those years, and yet…maybe I had. Maybe it was that small tender voice of young Ryan exploring in the woods near his home, that part of me who never really left and was quieted for so long. Maybe that voice did call out to me during those years when I had ventured too far from the group, the ones who really mattered, and myself. It just took me awhile to finally hear him.

"Who cooks for you? Who cooks for you all?" Maybe we all do. Maybe we all should.

# 12

## PRIDE BEFORE THE STORM

"You guys are rugged! It takes a lot of endurance and determination to do what you're doing, and I have a lot of respect for that. I wish you the best of luck."

These were the words of a gentleman I passed just before arriving in Daleville. Not only did they further boost my already high spirits from completing the Virginia Triple Crown the day before, but his words made me even more excited to enter Daleville. It was yet another of the many encouraging experiences I'd had with people on the trail, as opposed to many of the encounters in the "real world." This was what I had always hoped the trail would be, a connected and caring community, and I was a part of it. As these positive interactions mounted, I often wondered whether everyone ought to find their own version of "hiking the AT."

The people, however, were not what I looked forward to the most in Daleville. Like every visit to "civilization," it was the meals available that most occupied my mind, and the first itch I scratched was ambling into a Cracker Barrel and ordering the two largest breakfast meals on the menu. You can always tell a trail town by the reactions from servers. Do they stare at you strangely or knowingly when you saunter in with thirty-five pounds of possessions strapped to your back? Do they pretend not to notice the smell or give that familiar "I can get through this" smirk as they approach the table? And when you order enough food for a table of four for yourself, do they give you the mannerly "are you sure?" or jot it down and go about their business? Our server was certainly a thru-hiker veteran, taking our presence and orders without a flinch, all the way down to the side orders of biscuits and gravy and extra cheese and butter. She did chuckle after asking how BAMF wanted his eggs, and he returned, "Um… Good?"

Our ever-present hiker hunger quieted just long enough for BAMF, Woodpecker, a newly met thru-hiker named Bushwacker, and myself to clean ourselves up at the Super 8 room we secured, a rare-afforded luxury. We took a few-hour dip in the pool, then ordered pizza for lunch. Still hungry, we took advantage of a tip from a local that Three Li'l Pigs BBQ gave free banana bread pudding to thru-hikers.

Lying in bed that night at the Super 8, I thought about how difficult it would be to describe to a former me how impactful this trip had been. The feelings were as alien as they were transformative. I imagined the experience being similar to going your whole life believing you had perfect vision, then suddenly learning a new color, one that brought meaning to every other hue. How would I describe that? How would I convince former "me" of the importance? The more I thought about it, the less confident I was that I could, but the more convinced I was that I should try—not to the former me, of course, but to everyone. My words from meaningful-time tea a few nights earlier came back to me. "…I'm going to find a way to show them all this."

That night, at the end of my journal entry, I scribbled, "Scrambling Thru…a story about taking risks, going against the grain of life, and finding your passion and pursuing it."

The first time I saw this entry off-trail, I chuckled to myself in that protective way you do when remembering things said or promised in a moment of zeal. Who was I to write a book? Me, a thirty-something outdoor enthusiast still trying to figure out exactly what he wanted to do with his life. I had changed so much since jotting those words and knew I was still changing, still learning what it meant to "show them all this." But wasn't that the point? Wasn't that the whole point of the trail? To embrace growth as a journey, not some finished destination? To be okay just wandering, not sure where that wandering might take you? I still cringe a little at that first attempt at a title, "Scrambling Thru," but like each experience I've had since, it served its most important purpose. It was the increment I needed to bring me to the next moment and eventually this moment, the one I'm in now somewhere in the middle of all the moments of my life.

The morning after planning my literary future, I experienced my first real pull by a thing all thru-hikers eventually become acquainted with: "the vortex." Woodpecker and Bushwacker were already seated in the continental breakfast area when I arrived, coffees in front of them, mine in my hand from the compact drip machine in my room. We chatted about the day ahead, the immense pleasure of sleeping on a mattress the night before, where we hoped to reach that day, then back to the warm shower and how we could stand under it for an eternity. With every foray into the miles ahead, our internal compasses kept pointing us back to the comforts of the place we were. A half hour passed in a blink, and somehow, we each had fresh cups of coffee in front of us once again, another piece of toast and jam for me, a packaged blueberry muffin for Bushwacker.

Every town comes with the danger of being sucked into the vortex, the desire to delay your hike beyond your intended plans. The nearo of the previous day was something we all planned, but the morning was for getting ready and going, not lingering and waffling. I've heard stories of thru-hikers making it two-thirds of the way to Katahdin, only to be sucked into a vortex so strong they never left the hostel they happened to be staying in for one night. I even heard foreboding tales of some who began working where they stopped…they just never got up and left.

"Another cup?" asked Woodpecker.

I paused. "Better not."

We all nodded and got up to start packing for the return to the trail.

Thunderstorms were in the forecast for the next four days, and for almost the entirety of those four days, we hiked with nothing more than a drizzle, the sun coming and going as if the storm was always just around the next bend. But what initially felt like good luck devolved into wishing for the clouds to just open up and dump it out on us already. We were hiking a full day in humidity so thick you could see the haze. In the thick of it, I glimpsed Bushwacker swinging his trekking poles at unsuspecting shrubs further ahead and shared a smile with Woodpecker. A burger, fries, and a milkshake had at Middle

Creek Campground were nice distractions from constantly wanting to tear my clothes off and jump into the nearest water.

The next day, we came upon two gentlemen, one younger and one older, finishing a four-day section hike. They were preparing to leave the trail and had grossly over-planned food for their trip, leaving us with an endowment of Mountain House meals. There are few better food options on the trail than freeze-dried full meals packed with calories. Not only are they expensive but also very difficult to find at most resupply points. The fact that I now had my next few nights of food taken care of was an incredible bit of impromptu trail magic.

Day four since leaving the vortex of Daleville behind and the fourth day of forecasted rain, the clouds were not to be outdone by the previous three days of forecast busting. They disappeared entirely by noon and left the Blue Ridge mountains so hot that, even in the shade, I decided to stop and rest at a shelter. It was more accurately an oasis, sitting by a clear creek with a small swimming hole. Woodpecker, another thru-hiker named Carebear, and I had crossed the 800-mile mark that morning, so we decided to celebrate and cool down with a dip. Though the day was hot, the water in the creeks of the Blue Ridge Mountains never rose above frigid, even in the deepest part of summer. So, it was a surprise when I dipped my feet in and found a comfortable water temperature.

"Warmed by the rock," said Carebear, gesturing to the large, flat bluish-gray stone we were all sitting on.

"Nice! Nature's spa," I said, nodding. I hadn't considered just how powerful a well-positioned boulder could be, much like using a hot rock to boil and sterilize water for drinking.

"I think I'm going to stay here tonight," said Woodpecker. "Storms are definitely coming. Supposed to be pretty bad."

"Oh… Hopefully not as bad as the last few days," I smirked.

"Yeah, but these look legit," added Carebear seriously. "I'm staying behind too."

I smiled and wished them a good evening before making my way toward my planned stop.

It wasn't that I didn't believe the weather could turn violent; I just didn't have any fear of storms. By this point, I had been through a few on the trail. The first was a touch unsettling, but before long it was more therapeutic than scary, listening to the soft thunder rolling through the hills and valleys around you. There was a connectedness to nature that the storm brought, almost like a deep voice singing to you as you lay in your tent.

That evening, alone on the top of Bald Knob, nature was not serenading; it was pounding the very top of the mountains in violence. The lightning was so close, the air felt electric. Every flash brought an instant explosion that shook the earth and the very core of me. I believe my brain actually rattled in my head from the concussive force of heated air. I was terrified. From the first crack that tore across the sky, turning the dark sky into full daylight, I felt the sinking feeling in my stomach that I had made a very terrible mistake. When the floodwaters were unleashed a moment later, I did my best to master my fear and stride ahead assured that I would make it through, but that composure was tested by the smell of burning.

Like a campfire of pine logs had been built nearby, I was suddenly choked by the thick aroma of lightning-struck tree. I imagined the worst, a forest fire strong enough to burn through the torrential downpour. That was all I could take. With a sky alternating between soaked darkness, sizzling bright light, and the deafening roar, I adjusted my course and waded through a series of newly made rivers to the nearest shelter on the map.

Several times on that descent, I wondered if I had made a second terrible error, whether it would have been slightly safer to have pushed through as the storm burned itself out. I had to stop more than once to re-secure my shoes after having them nearly sucked from my feet by the increasingly mucky terrain. But I made it.

I kissed the inside wall of the shelter when I finally stood protected from the deluge of electricity and water. If I knew then what the rest of that night had in store, I might have punched the wood instead.

It was no surprise that I found the shelter empty. Given its location about a mile off the AT, it would have only been occupied by someone foolish enough to leave the much more robust shelter at the base of the mountain that afternoon to get caught in a terrible storm. And here that someone was, now listening to the same intensity of storm I'd begun the evening with on the bald. My fears were somewhat eased by the knowledge that this shelter was not new and must have been through many such storms. I promptly ignored the fact that these were maintained structures, often repaired between seasons due to sustained damage.

Somehow, I must have managed to fall asleep that night. I remember waking suddenly to the feeling of something falling on me, right in the middle of my sleeping bag.

Almost all shelters along the AT are known hideouts for the various non-human residents of the mountains, anything from harmless insects and spiders to birds and raccoons. This is one of the reasons I tended to avoid them, sleeping outside in my tent at shelter locations.

The most damaging by far of these denizens, and the most dangerous to humans, is the mouse. They destroy supplies in their search for calories and building materials for their homes. Worse still, they carry an assortment of diseases. As such, I investigated the ceiling of the shelter upon arrival. There were a few glowing eyes staring back at me, nothing like the infestations I'd read about.

When I woke that night, flinging a mouse from my midsection in the process, my first instinct was to grab my headlamp and reinspect the ceiling. There I found not a few pairs of glowing orbs but an entire mouse kingdom. Dozens. Maybe a hundred. What was only a small tuft of cotton in one corner of the pitched rafters upon arrival had turned into a cotton castle.

I panicked, shuffling through my supplies for whatever the mice had destroyed to create their new home, and to my surprise, found nothing had been touched or bitten. This made no sense. I scanned the four walls and corners of the space. I was still alone. Impossible. But it didn't matter. If I stayed, whatever I possessed that could be stolen eventually would be. So, during the dead of night, during the still raging storm, I packed my supplies and walked out into the loud and soaked woods. I found the highest mound of earth near the shelter and set up my tent, rehung my soaked clothes, and crumpled into a terrible sleep.

# 13

## HYPOTHETICALS

I felt low after the storm. My ego had put me in both dangerous and very inconvenient situations. Even though no one was
around to chide me, I felt the sharp prick of embarrassment
for the decision to leave the others and risk the night in the
storm. I also felt low; aside from the few nights of sickness, I
got maybe the worst sleep on the trail in that mouse kingdom
shelter.

I left camp that morning feeling like my feet weighed
double. I came over the bald I had attempted to sleep on the
night before, and a gust of cool breeze hit me right in the chest.
It was a refreshing breeze, the first of the last several days that
wasn't thick with moisture. The storm which had ruined my
night had also taken all the humidity and heat of the previous
four days with it. Suddenly, I didn't feel so low.

As I was leaving the bald, the sun peeked through the
clouds in the form of a bright glowing heart. I stopped and
basked in the moment's display and the rest of my gloomy
disposition melted away.

As I descended the bald a second time, now heading north,
I thought about how fickle moods are. Environment, fear, and

lack of sleep topped the list of things that soured my mood, but they were by no means all there was. Trail diet, the physical rigor I was putting my body through, the lack of contact with family and longtime friends—all these and certainly many more factors were lurking in the background of every feeling I had on the trail. There was comfort in the simple acknowledgment of this, a buffer between my current lightened mood and what could have dominated my thoughts that morning, the frustration of being frustrated, and the sadness about being low.

"You can't turn off the rain," I reminded myself. "But it never lasts forever."

The next few days, I tried to remind myself of this at every opportunity, each time, substituting the word rain for whatever the situation called for—a lack of energy, the hot sun, hunger. There were times when hunger felt like it might last forever. It was nice to know I was never alone in this. My collection of trail friends was always expanding, and recently I had met a guy called Cheese…from Wisconsin.

Cheese was the first person I met who was completely off the grid while on the trail, only communicating with the outside world via computers he could access in towns. I wondered if I should have built that into my own thru-hike and considered adopting it for the remainder. But for a variety of reasons, I didn't—not least of which was the fact that I was actively planning a meetup with my family and friends.

Cheese was also studying plants at university, and during lunch, he treated our skin ailments with a concoction he made out of Jewelweed, also known as Touch-me-not or Snapdragon. It worked. I was amazed at how powerful nature could be even in its simplest forms, and just how little I knew about it. While we were treating our ailments, we also conversed about the 1980s external frame pack of his father's that he carried, and the thing he missed the most while being on the trail was his grandmother's farm-to-table cooking.

The next day, Bushwacker, Woodpecker, a newly met thru-hiker called Speedo, and I broke our eighteen miles into two segments with a long-anticipated hitch to Devil's Backbone Basecamp at midday. The man who eventually stopped to pick us up in his flatbed truck offered to let two of us sit in the front bench seat with him, but his feisty wiener dog had other ideas. We were not disappointed as the wind cooled us in the back. The man gave us his phone number and offered to cart us back to the trail after lunch, which we happily accepted.

We never got any of this generous man's story, but I wondered what was going on in his day outside of the rides he offered. Before the trail, I might have felt guilty for accepting this charity, falling into the mindset that I was receiving a benefit while this kind man gained nothing. I had felt that way after my first few experiences with trail angels. But I learned that wasn't true; it never had been true—there was an immediate return on this man's investment to help his fellow human being, if nothing more than to drive away in his truck knowing that the world was still a place where people helped people, and that despite not knowing someone, you and that someone were still part of the same larger community. If you were in the same community, you could rely on each other. The trail helped me see that the concept of wealth being measured in dollars or possessions was a hollow and limited view. Wealth was measured in kindness and acts of service to each other, as well as the connectedness and experiences we shared.

The next day, BAMF and another thru-hiker called Blue Smurf joined my trail community. We made it into Waynesboro by the afternoon, and it was clear from the growing storm inside my stomach that my body needed another trail town. After the difficulty of the last several days, my mind needed it too. We secured calories at Stella Bella & Lucy's, an American breakfast and lunch joint downtown then I picked up a care package waiting for me at the post office from my mom. It was filled with her delicious homemade chocolate chip cookies which I was able to share with my current hiking mates. For the next few hours, BAMF and I decided to get laundry done and found ourselves sitting shirtless in an otherwise empty laundromat.

I was struck by the idea that it was only the fact that we were thru-hiking that made our current situation acceptable. Someone might come in and glance our way, and I could see that split second of uncertainty, bordering on unease. But it's likely they'd realize we were in town from the trail and would noticeably relax. Being a trail town, the locals of Waynesboro were used to thru-hikers. I couldn't expect the same from the inhabitants of Anywhere-else, USA. That made me appreciate the freedom of it all, all the more.

"I'm going to miss being on the trail," I said.

"Don't leave," BAMF joked.

We chuckled and were silent for a moment.

"Hm, maybe I won't," I pondered aloud. "The Pacific Crest Trail is starting to sound like a pretty good option for next year."

There were fewer chuckles after that.

The following day was a planned zero day in Waynesboro. We began with coffee and more conversation about what we would do after the trail. The idea of turning my attention to the Pacific Crest Trail gained inertia. We learned that this day, June 23rd, was Canada's National Day of Remembrance for victims of terrorism, so we honored that with BAMF with a few drinks. As I lay in bed that night at the Quality Inn, I visualized myself on the other side of the country in a very different set of mountains, doing the same things I was doing now. It felt right. As I look back on those thoughts now, I don't know whether that was because I felt I needed more time to decide what after-trail life should look like, or if I thought there was a version of my future that was never going to be "after-trail".

This dominated my thoughts the next several days as we left Waynesboro behind and ventured into the beautiful, bear-rich section of the AT that ran through Shenandoah National Park. We saw several bears and were even asked, "Who cooks for us?" by another Barred Owl. Another bird was not so kind with its call, one known as a Whip-poor-Will. Perched within close distance to our tents, this nocturnal bird spent the entire night screaming, "Whip poor Will, whip poor Will." No amount of shushing and slapping the canvas of my tent could scare this creature off or reduce its desire for us to flog some poor guy named Will. I rested very little that night.

Not long before crossing the 900-mile mark, we met a trail maintenance worker who congratulated us on coming this far from Springer Mountain. This made me feel like we had crossed an invisible threshold, that we had gone far enough now that people would begin to congratulate rather than question us. I was proud of myself and also felt the need to guard against that feeling of accomplishment, with so much of the trail still lying ahead.

"Do you know how long we've known each other?" BAMF asked me.

Before he answered, there was already something in the way he phrased his question that made me realize he was not just another fellow thru-hiker but a friend. I began doing the mental math from when we walked through the archway together at the approach trail to now, when he answered for me.

"Nine hundred miles. That's how long."

"Nine hundred miles." I smiled and nodded. That was right…and more meaningful than any number of days or years.

A couple days later, after setting up my tent for the evening, I was sitting with a couple other thru-hikers I'd hiked with off and on, one called Skittles and the other, 2 Chairz. BAMF and I had separated again by our differing paces as we had many times since Springer, but I knew we would come back together. Either he would wait for me somewhere, or I would wait for him.

2 Chairz asked if we could hike with one celebrity, who it would be. My first thought was, I wouldn't. I'd rather hike it with the people I had been hiking it with. I pictured BAMF and Woodpecker, Red Bull and all the others, including the two beside me just then.

Skittles said Jim Carrey, specifically his character from Dumb and Dumber, and 2 Chairz chose Paul Rudd with a voiceover from Morgan Freeman, which I thought was a nice touch. It took me a while to come up with a suitable famous person, and in the end, I stretched the rule of "celebrity" a bit.

I pictured myself in my former life, a time when I was somewhat aware of movies coming out and who the famous actors were. In this image, I was back at the office sitting at my desk in the final weeks at my corporate job. That's when it hit me, I knew exactly who I would hike the Appalachian Trail with.

Above the desk was a quote I'd hung the day after I put in my notice. There were several times when a colleague would enter my office with the usual quick, frantic steps of that environment, then stop in silence. I would wait, smiling at my computer screen, waiting for the inevitable sigh that would always follow. The words that prompted these responses read as follows:

The Dalai Lama was once asked, "What surprises you most about humanity?"

*"Man, because he sacrifices his health in order to make money. Then he sacrifices money to recuperate his health. And then he is so anxious about the future that he does not enjoy the present; the result being that he does not live in the present or the future; he lives as if he is never going to die, and then dies having never really lived."*

# 14

## A ROAMING HOME

I like to believe that at a certain point, the 550 miles of Virginia would begin to wear on any thru-hiker to a level that is no longer easily ignored. When the "green tunnel" and "Virginia blues" become your reality, you want nothing more than a different reality. For me, this moment came during my last four days in Virginia. Most of that stretch had turned into a blur with only punctuations of lucidity. I have to rely heavily on my journals to remember exactly what had happened in those days.

After departing Shenandoah National Park, Skittles and I made our way to Front Royal, a quaint town where we were able to fully resupply and grab, not one, but two dinners—one in town, the other we brought back to the hostel for a late-night snack. The rest of that day was filled, intentionally, with a whole lot of nothing. To be fair, that describes the vast majority of my time at each resting place. Rubbing calves and ankles, and stretching, sitting in a hot bath or under a hot shower if available, eating and chatting idly, or meaningfully if tea was involved—this way of resting allowed myself to recuperate in ways I'd never had to do before hiking the Appalachian Trail, while at the same time, not having to recuperate in many other ways I'd always had to do before hiking the trail.

So, that's what I did into the evening and until bedtime at Mountain Home Cabin, run by a past thru-hiker called Possible. The next morning, I saw that my coffee mug read, "Everything is Possible." It was just the right amount of corny paired perfectly with caffeine. Those words saw us out the door as we set out again into the green blur.

I held my mind as closely as I could to the mindset that like the rain, this too would eventually come to an end. This was interrupted by my tenth bear sighting, a thing never boring which gave the body fresh adrenaline for the next mile or so. I also met a couple new thru-hikers who mentioned that a few "May Starters" were catching up, and I thought about how that sounded like a reference to a rare and different species.

The AT seemed to know we needed a change and decided to give us the state line early. We had been looking forward to (and somewhat dreading) a stretch called "the roller-coaster"—a difficult thirteen-mile section, during which, one climbs and descends over thirty-five hundred feet of elevation and crosses the 1,000-mile mark of the trail. By the time we neared the beginning of the roller-coaster, I had psyched myself up so much, I no longer felt the Virginia Blues at all. Then Skittles had an accident. He wasn't hurt, but there was a casualty involved.

This was much like one of those situations involving a car and a squirrel, the kind every driver can immediately picture—the squirrel sits on the road teetering back and forth between crossing and staying put, only to leap in front of the vehicle at the last minute, and literally, its last minute on earth. In this case, the squirrel was a mouse, and the vehicle was Skittles. We never saw the poor guy until the damage had already been done.

I heard Skittles curse behind me, and by the time I turned around, there was the mouse, belly up, taking a few last quick breaths, bleeding from its head. Without a doubt, this creature was suffering until its inevitable death, so Skittles ended its suffering with a rock, then dug a hole to one side of the trail and buried it under the rock.

After spending so much time immersed in and connected with the beauty and purity of nature, to snuff a portion out, even a tiny portion, feels something like a part of yourself dying. I tried telling myself it was just a mouse, but I felt a sinking pain and loss as soon as I thought it. What if I was just a mouse to someone? Instead of trying to minimize what had happened, I accepted it, feelings and all. I cried silently for a while. We were all a little quiet that day, our minds on the little mouse. In that simple way, I think we honored its life. No life is too small.

The moment I had been craving for many days arrived, the end of the 550 miles of green, and we crossed the Virginia state line. I felt something akin to guilt when we left the Commonwealth State behind, like Virginia had turned into a struggle and meant I'd somehow not given it a fair shake. After crossing, I stopped and thought about my experiences and decided to say a silent thanks. I held no grudge for the "green tunnel" and knew it held importance for the AT itself, as well as myself. Every experience was shaping me, and I was grateful. I was ready for something different, another new experience.

We camped that night at Keys Gap, about five miles from another place I'd circled on my trail map long before setting out. That next day, I officially became the 1,305[th] Northbound thru-hiker to cross through Harpers Ferry, West Virginia, the unofficial halfway point of the trail. Before entering town, I stopped at the ATC Harper's Ferry Visitor Center, had my picture taken, wrote all my information in the registry, and cemented my place in Appalachian Trail history.

Arriving in town, I was instantly struck by the charm, more than I had expected from the descriptions in all the thru-hike guidebooks I'd read. The houses were right out of a Thomas Kinkade painting—streets paved with cobblestone and historic streetlamps lining the sidewalks. This was a place I knew I wanted to spend some time exploring and decided the next day would be a fourth zero day.

Things like months and days tend to slip out of mind while on the trail, and unfortunately for me, I didn't realize until that moment I had wandered into this quaint town on July 4th weekend. Not a single room, bed, cot, or Ryan-sized patch of floor was available for rent within a twenty-mile radius. I usually liked to splurge on zero days to maximize rest and recuperation, but I was forced to readjust my expectations and accept a less-desirable option.

Knowing I could always stealth-camp somewhere in the nearby woods, I decided to table the dilemma and get to know this amazing town. My father, who was following my adventure through text updates, informed me he had a colleague who happened to be visiting family nearby. I decided to call him. My father had never been to Harper's Ferry and knew nothing about it, but his colleague, Matt, and his wife, Whitney, were staying about twenty-five minutes away visiting their parents.

Within a few minutes, my father had communicated with Matt and Whitney, and a couple of true angels of the trail were on their way to pick up Skittles and me. The rest of that day could not have been better had I planned the entire time myself. On the way out of town, we stopped for roadside barbecue, then enjoyed the fantastic views offered by a local brewery. Matt's parents met us there, and the rest of the afternoon, we shared stories of our hike.

Matt's mother had read a few thru-hiking books and seemed academically engrossed in everything we told of. It was nice to have someone who hadn't hiked the trail not put on a face of "why would you ever do that?" immediately after meeting us.

After a quick resupply at a grocery store, we were brought back to their home where we were treated like traveling princes. We enjoyed hot showers, during which I began to smell the amazing meal our hosts were preparing—home-made pizza with portabellas, lamb, and locally made sausage. When we were truly stuffed, we retired to the backyard in time for a showing of fireflies. I had never seen that many and it was honestly something I would have paid money for. Matt's parents washed our clothes while we rested. In the span of a short afternoon and evening, I felt like I had gained more family.

The next day, I was torn. I had planned for some time to take a zero day in Harpers Ferry, and a large part of me wanted to explore the cobbled streets and pop into the many shops, cafes, and galleries... And yet, for the first time on a zero day, I was anxious to get back on the trail. It was as if the intense dose of domestic civility had reminded me of what I was missing.

In the end, I decided to stick with my original plans to remain a full day in Harpers Ferry and was glad for it. I did my best to relax as I strolled its streets, a very different pace from hiking. I ate some good food and even decided that I could see myself returning to that quaint town. But as I lay down that night, I wanted nothing more than returning to the trail. Like a vortex, the pull was strong. And it was a great feeling, knowing I was on the right path, and wanting to be doing the very thing that I *was* doing.

Before I fell asleep, I fondly remembered I had something else to look forward to besides getting back on the trail. I would be seeing my family in three days. I decided to look at the remaining mileage in the morning and form a plan.

# 15

## HURRY UP AND REST

*I'm seeing my family in three days*, I thought with a smile. *Wait! I see my family in three days!*

Panic set in at the first glance of my trail guide that morning. That couldn't be right. I read and re-read, each time checking against the date on my phone, July 3rd, 2017. I would be meeting my family on July 5th...78.6 miles away.

Up to that point, my longest single day of hiking was about twenty-five miles. I'd only done that twice, and those two almost-twenty-five-mile days were separated by a week. To reach my family, I would need to average more than that, three days in a row.

In my off-trail life, I focus a lot on staying present, focused, and fully engaged in what I'm doing. This was a mindset I had no concept of in my pre-trail corporate life. I was first exposed to it during my preparation for the hike and applied it to great benefit during those arduous miles. Now, whether I'm in conversation, performing a productivity-related task, or simply resting, I try to assume a meditation-like level of concentration on that one thing. So much of this relies on a mindset of slowing down and moving at a pace both mentally and physically that allows me to notice all the details of what I'm doing and remain immersed in an appreciation for that thing. The next three days on the Appalachian Trail, as I feverishly tried to arrive on time to see my family, I was not moving at a pace of being present.

Day one of three, I raced from Harpers Ferry, West Virginia to the Ensign Cowall Shelter, just outside a small town called Smithsburg, 31.1 trail miles away. I rolled into camp after the sun had set and surprised Skittles, who had left Harpers Ferry the day before and had arrived only that afternoon. Of that day, I can only recall crossing into Maryland, that my feet and legs hurt, and that if ever you were planning to hike over thirty miles in a day on the AT, Maryland was the place to do it. By AT standards, it was relatively flat, the weather was mild, and the trail was well-maintained. I'd heard that Maryland was known for its great variety of native roses, which grow in many regions of its varied landscape. If there were any along the trail that day, I did not stop to smell them.

The second of three days was considerably more memorable. To begin with, it was Independence Day, and the trail was adorned with various small flags, streamers, and the leftover paper from an assortment of firecrackers I heard echoing throughout my hike. Then there was the trail magic which happened three separate times. Not far from camp, the first bit of magic was understated but useful, a simple cache of water on the side of the trail. I stopped, drank down the bottle, and continued on, happy I was not having to dip into my own stores for a time.

However, my expectations were significantly exceeded when I stumbled upon a group of trail angels. My nose was well ahead of my eyes, but my whole being was enlivened when I saw the tent set up with hot dogs, a crock full of sloppy joe, sodas, water, brownies, and cookies. If you had asked me to write down a list of the top ten food items I would want to see at an on-trail pop-up tent, every one of these would have been on it.

Following that joyful event, the trail ran along a park, and there was a couple sitting at a table offering Capri Sun pouches and Starburst candies. Not as robust as the hot dog tent, perhaps, but still a welcome and delightfully refreshing addition to a second very long day of hiking.

Not long after crossing into Pennsylvania, consequently across the Mason Dixon Line into the "North," I surprised a few more thru-hikers with my presence, this time, BAMF, Roadrunner, and a couple familiar faces from camping together in Shenandoah National Park, Roadrunner and Keep Up.

I can't say that the stretch from Ensign Cowall Shelter to Quarry Gap Shelter found me any more present than the previous. There were no epiphanies, no revelations beyond the trail magic happily experienced. I didn't note the subtle differences in the landscape around me or spend much time celebrating the holiday or the additional state line crossed. But I performed my task admirably and achieved my goal. These became my first and only back-to-back thirty-mile days, and I'm happy to say, they were also the only thirty-mile days of my entire hike.

I was emotional arriving at the shelter that night, not only because I had accomplished such a feat of hiking but because my friends were there, BAMF in particular. And that also meant that the next day, when I got to spend time with my family, I would get to introduce them to my trail family. In such a short time, these strangers I had met walking on a two-foot-wide patch of dirt had become like related family to me. I couldn't put them in the same category as my other friends because we shared a bond that could only be created through this common experience.

Because of my record-setting back-to-back days, I was left with a reasonable 17.2 miles left to reach my family on the third day. July 5th is a much more clearly remembered day. I reached the official halfway point of the Appalachian Trail. The trail changes in distance year-after-year, so the halfway point must be moved, but at the time I was hiking, the sign read 1,094.9 miles. I took the obligatory selfie, and in my usual fashion of celebrating milestones, I made a large "50%" out of nearby rocks.

When I finished placing the smooth stones, I stood over them and teared up. I had celebrated all such moments like this, but this one felt different. That it was emotional was of course no surprise. But this held a significance I hadn't expected. Had I truly believed I would make it that far? Halfway? There might have been some part of me that expected to find a reason to quit before making it to such a significant distance. I think it was the part that wondered if quitting my marriage was a glimpse into who I really was.

I cried—not a little—at the halfway point, then felt a rush of relief that I hadn't quit, and relief that I had decided to give this adventure a chance in the first place. Then in some small way, the next half of the upcoming journey felt less scary, like I had arrived at the peak of a great mountain, and only a gentle slope down the other side remained. With a single step, there was more trail behind me than in front.

Each step felt a little lighter as we walked on. I was glad to have pushed through the previous two days and could then focus on returning to being present for my family. When their cabin came into view, I stopped and took a deep breath and tried to steel myself against the flood of emotions I knew was coming. I never had a chance. I heard "Who is that, Clive?" in a familiar voice. "Is that Uncle Ryan?"

My twin sister was speaking to her three-year-old son, Clive, and was standing beside my mom. As my nephew jogged toward me, I thought about how I hadn't seen family since before starting this journey, and when Clive saw me last, I was still trying to pretend I loved a career I hated, how I had just walked almost eleven hundred miles to be in this moment, 1,100 miles that separated me from the person I was and brought the person I was now to my family, the person they would soon get to know in a hurry.

I choked up, receiving those hugs, and choked up again seeing my dad and brother and his family, most of whom were wearing "Breathtaking Journey" shirts. It was more than I was ready for, and I asked as politely as I could to excuse myself. I had walked from Georgia to Pennsylvania, and I still needed a little more time. There was something called "the ½ gallon challenge" at the Pine Grove Furnace General Store just steps away from the cabin. This was a staple for thru-hikers at the halfway point and could perhaps provide a good buffer to give myself time to get my emotions back under control.

In the end, there was no amount of time or focus or ounces of ice cream that could diminish the immense support and outpouring of love my family gave me. They had come to see me halfway through the craziest decision of my life, and I loved them more than I could say and gave in to the abundant feelings I felt.

I spent the remainder of that day and the next lounging, eating, and telling stories, with my family telling embarrassing stories about me to my new friends they'd just met. I had to take breaks from smiling and laughing to rub my sore face muscles, and a pile of tissues was always forming next to me. My fellow thru-hikers, collectively representing five different countries, were given places to sleep on the screened porch of the cabin. Coffee and bagels were prepared in the morning we were to leave.

As I sat sipping and eating in the early light, I smiled, realizing that of all the incredible trail magic I'd experienced, none was so magical as the warm generosity and love of family.

# 16

## THE TRUE HEROES

Leaving my family was just as tearful as meeting them. But I was ready to be on my way, ready to continue my journey to Katahdin, my journey to self-discovery. At the entrance to Pine Grove Furnace State Park, I noticed an ATC museum and decided to stop in before putting in miles for the day. There were informational writings and images about the history of the trail. Standing out most to me was one of the Katahdin summit signs from past years. There have been many over the years, and this one had already welcomed years' worth of thru-hikers to the peak. I walked right up to it and felt goose-bumps cover my arms and neck. I reached out to touch its worn wood but stopped. A feeling came over me, a realization that I needed to wait until I reached its young replacement in Maine.

I didn't hike remarkably far that day, just shy of nineteen miles, but a solid day compared to most in terms of distance. But my focus was elsewhere—it was my first full day of hiking after crossing the halfway point of the trail, and a smile kept tugging at my cheeks. I'd feel it and shake my head in giddy disbelief. I didn't fight it. After all, I had taken all those steps to get to this point, I had every reason to be happy.

The next day was slightly longer, a twenty-two-mile leg to Cove Mountain Shelter. Before embarking, I treated myself to breakfast at Cafe 101, a charming little cafe with a warm and inviting atmosphere and views of the picturesque Children's Lake running the entire length of the town of Boiling Springs, Pennsylvania. The smells of fresh coffee and steaming pancakes and bacon were welcoming. Historic photos of the downtown adorned the dining room. Perhaps more pleasant than all this was the fact that it no longer surprised me that I noticed all these little details, the kind my busy mind never would have in my previous life.

I ordered a breakfast plate with a cup of coffee, and both were as good as they smelled. Other hikers trickled in as I ate and followed my example. Conversations ensued, including topics of the beautiful weather, the strangeness of deciding to hike more than 2,100 miles, and things we looked forward to on the road ahead. That morning, I sat with two thru-hikers named Pawki and Ski Poles.

As breakfast wound down, Pawki asked why I was out here on the AT. Having already answered that question more times than I could tally, I gave him the packaged response—the departure from my corporate job, the divorce, the desire to find myself again. Pawki listened intently, and when I was finished, told me he admired my courage. Just about everyone on the trail had said something similar, some variation of how scary it must have been to make such drastic changes, to leave so much security to then start over from scratch. Although I had heard these words so many times, something was different this time.

"It isn't scary, really," I surprised myself by saying and hoped I hadn't come off rude.

"No?"

"Sorry, I mean...I guess I'm just not scared anymore."

I had to do an internal check to see if what I had just said was true, and sure enough, I was calm. I wasn't scared at all. This was exactly where I was meant to be, and I was grateful for the opportunity to pursue my dreams wherever they led. At present, that was out of Boiling Springs and toward a lot of cornfields.

When I left the cozy cafe, I carried with me the well-wishes of the entire Cafe 101 staff and the handful of thru-hikers I'd met over coffee and eggs. The first few miles were a gently sloping, clear trail. Cornfields, by design, don't tend to be planted in severe elevation. But soon enough, I became keenly aware that they also aren't planted in the shade. Approaching the middle of July, as I walked through the miles of maize, I found myself returning to my water bottle more often than at any other portion of the trail. I was craving a distraction, and Pennsylvania provided.

*Bang!* I heard coming from somewhere up ahead. *Bang! Bang!* Those were unmistakably gunshots, and I was undoubtedly in the middle of nowhere. I stopped and scanned the nearby area and found the distinctive white blazes.

"Do they let people hunt this close to the trail?" I asked myself nervously out loud.

*Bang! Bang! ... Bang!* Another trio of shots rang out, and I ducked fearing I might be the target of a rogue property owner or hunter mistaking me for a deer.

A moment later, my chest eased as I recognized I was likely near a shooting range. This explanation was comforting enough to get my feet moving again but not enough that I didn't flinch or duck instinctively with every echoing crack of gun blast as I hurried to put as much distance between myself and that place as possible. I could even smell the gunpowder in the air long after I heard the last echo.

The next day, just three miles after departing Cove Mountain Shelter, the scare was rekindled when I smelled something burning. I waited for the sound of shotgun fire to come blistering across the trail. The moment was short-lived and replaced with something much more pleasant. This was the smell of charcoal.

As the band of trail angels came into view, their smiling faces lifted my spirits, and the smell of sizzling meat hurried my steps. Like so many others, they weren't there for money or to be mentioned in a local newspaper, nor to impress their friends. They just wanted to help hikers have a better trail experience and maybe hear a few of their stories.

After so much altruism on the trail, I thought about the tendency we humans have to grow numb to things you've experienced a number of times. People move near the beach or the mountains, and within a few years, they stop going. I'm no stranger to this phenomenon. During my pre-trail life, I lived in Hoboken while working in the bustling metropolis of New York City. I was there for four years and rarely made time for the amenities of the largest cultural center in the world. But there was something about the numerous instances of trail angels that seemed to transcend this numbing experience. I don't know if it was just one of the many life-affirming effects of the trail or something else—kindness perhaps. Maybe kindness is something, if we'd just choose it more often, that never gets old.

My unexpected trail-side barbecue fueled me to twenty-five miles that day, and I was extra thankful for the nourishment when I became aware that I had arrived in the portion of the trail known as "Rocksylvania". The harsh, craggy terrain of Rocksylvania was a sharp contrast to the previous many miles of cornfields. This tendency for great and sudden changes in terrain was one of the most rewarding aspects of the AT. One moment, you could be engaging in a leisurely walk along flat ground, and the next, you emerge into a place with a reputation for being able to "break you" physically and spiritually.

I had been ambivalently aware of my approach to this crucible of the trail days before it arrived but hadn't begun thinking about it in earnest until my feet landed on its first gray boulders. I was guarded at first, slowly going along, preserving my energy for what was heralded as one of the most difficult and injury-causing stretches of the entire trail. As the miles continued, I wondered at how well I was handling it. There was no "breaking" of my body and spirit. To the contrary, I was striding along, hopping between relatively flat rocks that reminded me of many other challenging portions that didn't question my resolve.

By the end, I found myself somewhat disappointed. "Rocksylvania" was a beautiful hike, and one that would continue on for days of fantastic sights and experiences. But it wasn't, to me, the brutal slog it had been made out to be. My hiking legs had really kicked in by this point, and I don't want to disparage anyone else's experience, but I wonder whether this was an example of how we often fear future events, building them up in our minds; and when we finally reach them, realize that the time spent fearing them was far worse than the experience itself. I can't say that I ever truly feared "Rocksylvania," but had more looked forward to an intense challenge. Instead of the challenge, I found myself enjoying the increased focus that many strewn rocks forced upon me and an increased presence among the Zen-like scattering of boulders my balancing ankles attempted to navigate. There was a necessary attention required, but soon, I wasn't focusing but sort of gliding along.

There were a few moments as Rocksylvania continued on when the weight of my pack became noticeable, and I was tempted to slip into a mindset of drudgery. I wondered if I had moved past the honeymoon phase of the trail, where hiking becomes work. But something would always interrupt those feelings—a butterfly or a still pool in a stream, a bit of cool shade or another trail angel. When I wanted to grumble, these little observances would draw me back in. Yes, my pack was heavy, but I needed everything in it to be there. The experience I had in the next town I visited gave me more reason to be grateful than any previous on the trail.

Port Clinton was a nice town, but not one I would have circled on the map were it not for a person I was to meet there, Ed. I had connected with Ed on Facebook and had plans to meet him that evening for dinner. Ed had been following my hike and my mission to raise awareness for cystic fibrosis, a disease that had affected his life in a very personal way. By the time I arrived in Port Clinton, my path had joined back up with BAMF and Keep Up, and Ed insisted that he wanted to treat us all to dinner.

It was a difficult thing for me to wrap my mind around at first, the idea that this man, who had come no short distance to meet me and had a disease that created a constant battle for normalcy, was going to treat us to dinner…and not the other way around. I offered multiple times to get the bill, and each time he adamantly refused, telling me it was his honor.

I had never anticipated moments like this when I first got involved with the Cystic Fibrosis Foundation with my brother or when I made the decision to dedicate my thru-hike to CF. It had simply seemed like the thing to do. As I listened to Ed at dinner tell me how excited he was to be a part of my adventure, I couldn't help but feel a little guilty. Even though my reasons for volunteering in the first place were to help people like Ed, I couldn't hide from the fact that it was also a part of the "program" of being in the corporate world. I was rubbing elbows with others in the community, making connections, becoming "important." I could hide from that back then when everyone's choices around me seemed to be angled for career growth. Now, in the stillness of my mind on the trail, I wrestled with my intentions, whether they had always been as well-placed as I thought they were now.

There was no doubt about Ed's intentions. He was nothing but excitement and gratitude that we had come to meet him and that I had created the Breathtaking Journey in the first place. I smiled at his compliments, trying not to feel embarrassed. Then he said something that struck deeply—he said it was people like me that made people like him feel not so alone, that while it was so important to have support from other people suffering with CF, solely being a part of that community felt isolated in the broader world community. But when people outside the CF community acknowledged the struggle and showed up with support, a bridge to the rest of the world became real. He felt seen and heard and understood.

I sat there humbled. Whether my intentions had always been pure or if they would never be perfect, it didn't matter. What was far more important was that I had done what little I could.

After dinner, Ed drove us to a nearby supermarket to resupply, then dropped us at our hotel. Me and my fellow thru-hikers stayed up late talking about how much that day had meant to each of us, how we saw the world just a little differently and saw ourselves a little differently within it.

The next day, we were joined on the trail by Colleen, another person enduring the trials of CF. She and a friend hiked out of Port Clinton with us, taking on a difficult stretch of rough terrain. She would not allow CF to stop her from experiencing the joys and wonders of an adventure and stayed with us for 7.5 miles before turning back. I couldn't help marveling at the incredible strength and resilience of this community. Despite the challenges they faced, they pushed themselves to the limit. I was honored to be a part of their journey.

That night when I switched my phone off airplane mode to check for messages, I smiled when I saw Pat's name pop up. Pat's a long-time friend I made volunteering with the CF community; his three-year-old daughter at the time has CF. He would send me weekly motivation videos of her urging "Ryan-buddy" to "keep on trucking." I watched the video and lay there beaming.

"Tell her I will," I texted back. And I did.

# 17
## WALKING HOME

After putting a day between ourselves and Port Clinton and the incredible examples of Ed and Colleen, it was difficult to keep my mind on the trail and off the fact that my home state of New Jersey was just two days away. The climb out of Lehigh Gap that morning was one of BAMF's and my favorite sections of the hike. The terrain was steep and rugged, demanding a focused determination from every step. The trail was marked by rocks and roots, while dense vegetation and towering trees surrounded us.

Climbing higher, occasional clearings offered glimpses of the surrounding landscape. Looking down into the valley, I could see the Lehigh River winding its way through the terrain, a ribbon of shimmering water that contrasted with the lush greenery around it. The mountains on either side of the valley created a natural amphitheater, their slopes showcasing the rugged beauty of the area.

Reaching the top of the gap, I paused to catch my breath and take in the view. The vista was expansive, with the valley stretching out below me with rolling hills in the distance. It was a reminder of the vastness and resilience of the natural world, not the picture-perfect scene of a postcard, a raw and authentic representation of the Appalachian landscape and testament to the trail's ability to challenge and reward.

But as we made our descent from the gap, no valley crossed or crest reached kept my mind from turning homeward. My focus on the trail was returned as we hiked through two days of back and forth between drizzle and torrential downpour, but even between the slippery stretches where focus was of paramount importance, my attention would wander to the bridge over the Delaware River and cross back into familiar territory, wondering what it would be like after coming so far through the unknown.

Instead of camping in the rain and going another twenty-four hours in wet clothes, we decided to spring for the rare luxury of a hotel that night. I connected with a close friend in Stroudsburg, and they offered to pick BAMF and me up and transport us to a hotel when we arrived in town. That evening, I had a nice dinner with my friend. I wasn't back in New Jersey, but meeting her felt like the first taste of home, and made my soon-to-be arrival feel so close, I ached for it.

Afterwards, BAMF and I met for drinks. We arrived at the bar and ordered a couple beers, and to our surprise, two girls already sitting struck up a conversation with us. We were both clean, hygienically speaking, but still sporting gnarly trail beards, not to mention wearing trail attire of short mesh shorts and crocs with socks. We chatted politely for a brief time until thru-hiking was mentioned. Their faces immediately went from kind interest to quiet repulsion. There was a long pause with wordless glances between the two, though their looks said it all. "Yikes…how do we get out of this?" from one. The other, "Follow my lead." Then in as few polite words as possible, excuses were made, and the two removed themselves to the furthest open table in the establishment. We laughed this off, enjoying our refreshing beverages and a new conversation topic of how many people couldn't understand, or didn't want to understand, our journey. Like the "working" man I'd run into with Knots who said our problem was we didn't know how to work, these girls had come to their own conclusion without knowing us. How quick we are to judge what we don't understand? I wondered if pre-trail Ryan would have formed the same conclusion of us sitting there in our trail clothes.

Leaving the hotel the next morning, my mind was right back to where it had been previously. The concept of being present on the trail, valuable as it was, held no interest for me. I was firmly set on the fact that this was my last day in Pennsylvania, and soon I would be staring across the water toward the glistening shores of the place I called home. I had enjoyed PA, with its rocky, steep, and winding paths. At no point did I feel the intense fatigue which had dogged me in earlier portions of the trail. Instead, PA had provided a moderately strenuous and beautiful section, and despite rumors or more treacherous wandering, there was nothing ultimately to fear. I had yet to face the fabled Whites of New Hampshire.

But these ponderings of whether my relative ease in Pennsylvania was due to increased endurance or an elevated energy of nearing home, they were interrupted. After nearly eighteen miles that day, I crested the peak of Mt. Minsi and stopped to take in my first view of New Jersey. The Delaware River separated the foothills below where I stood from their larger siblings at the base of Mt Tammany on the other side, the first of the New Jersey peaks I'd soon be skirting. I was frozen on that mountaintop, and I began to feel in a way I never had. I couldn't describe it at the time, and I'm not sure I can now. A simple thought kept repeating itself. "I just walked all the way home from Georgia."

We stopped that evening just shy of the NJ state line so in the morning, all we had left was to cross the bridge. The following day, we made our way to the bridge, and on the Pennsylvania end, I was forced to halt as an eagle flying over the bridge dove close to the waters of the Delaware. For me, fireworks exploding or jets flying in formation wouldn't be a better celebration marking our arrival. I watched the Eagle until it flew out of view, then stepped onto the bridge.

A few close friends had driven out to meet us and cross with me. They brought coffee and doughnuts, and those were welcome adornments to the moment but not so impactful as their presence. There was something in this moment shared that felt like meeting all over again. They hadn't changed as far as I could tell, yet they were completely new to me. I saw them with such a pure feeling of joy, like I was getting to know them, yet knew they were already my people. This experience, and the thought of hiking through familiar territory just ahead, reminds me now of the concept I have come across called Shoshin, a practice developed by Zen Buddhists. The idea is to adopt a "beginner's mind," to see each moment, person, or thing in your life each time as though you are seeing them for the first time, to appreciate them for what they are and what they mean to you each day anew. It's a way of finding perpetual gratitude and wonder in a world that is so easy to take for granted. If every moment is new, then each experience is one you've never had. As Maya Angelou said, "This is a wonderful day. I have never seen this one before."

I felt nothing but gratitude as my friends joined BAMF, Keep Up, and me for a few extra miles so they could celebrate the 1,300-mile mark with us. One of those friends was Tim, whom I had formed a relationship with when starting volunteer work with the CF Foundation. Tim also had CF, so when we celebrated the 1,300-mile mark, he and I stood for a photo holding up the Breathtaking Journey flag between us.

After celebrating, I hugged each of my friends goodbye, and we continued hiking for another eighteen miles. Those miles and the ones I hiked the next day reminded me just how beautiful New Jersey is. So many people, when they hear the words New Jersey, they might think of the Jersey Shore or the big cities like Newark and Trenton, much like people conflate the skyscrapers of New York City into the whole New York State, missing its Adirondack Mountains and pristine Finger Lakes. The Kittatinny Ridge in New Jersey offers some of the best views and most incredible countryside of the entire trail. Coming down from the Kittatinny Ridge, I ran into an older gentleman named Clyde, and we hiked together for a stretch. A New Jersey native himself, we chatted about these perceptions of our state and how it must be true that every state has some unfair misconception. I thought about how many people in these great cities, like Newark or New York, who have never left the glittering bubbles and high energy, the constant activity and noise, and how they have no idea this much natural beauty is so close by.

"I'm going to show them this," I told the older gentleman. "I'm going to find a way to bring them here, to give them this experience."

"If that's all you ever did," he said, "you will have done a lot."

Another day in New Jersey, a friend brought me breakfast on the trail, and another delivered lunch. I don't think I can express just how moving it was to be able to call my off-trail friends trail angels.

I then came to a stretch I had hiked many times as a child, one running directly behind my high school in Vernon, New Jersey. From there, I hiked across the locally iconic Appalachian Trail Boardwalk, which traversed a low-lying area, then along Heaven Hill Farm, where colleagues of my father met BAMF and me with homemade cider donuts. As sweet of a surprise as that was, an even sweeter one waited for us a few miles later. A young boy with CF, Marty, and his mom had come to see me on the trail. Seeing his face glow when I pulled out the Breathtaking Journey flag made the entire hike worth the effort. After the meeting, Marty's grandmother sent me a text message:

Dear Ryan, as Marty's grandmother I have felt hope instead of fear as I watched your progress along this gorgeous trail. With each post, I thought someone is now thinking about CF and that person may hold the key to saving my precious grandson. Marty suffers from the worst form of CF with very rare mutations. A cure is far off for him. As I watched a strong young man make this incredible journey, I dreamed of Marty being able to do it one day as well, unfettered, without hours of vests and treatments. Please continue to champion our cause and thank you for sharing your wonderful adventure.

That evening, after finishing our miles for the day, my parents picked BAMF and me up and took us to a place where we could introduce my hiking partner to real New Jersey pizza, and then to my home, my actual home, for two zero days. In the quiet comfort of my childhood home, I realized just how much of a friend BAMF had become. Not only had he learned to speak an enormous amount of English during our miles together, coming from almost none at the beginning of the trail, but he had also come to know me unlike anyone off the trail ever had. He had been a witness as I became the person I always was beneath the layers of the corporate world, a person curious and free to wander. That human-to-human connection on the trail is hard to describe. In such a relatively short period of time, you can know someone better than those you've known all your life.

I didn't journal those two days at home. I took a break from everything: from the trail, from the future, from the past—everything. I just let myself be. My parents invited friends and family over to celebrate the miles I had hiked and the journey forward. The outpouring of support was a nourishment unlike any food I'd encountered in any trail town, and I hadn't known just how much I needed it.

My parents drove BAMF to the airport, where he would be flying off to a wedding in Africa. It impacted me to see him leave. This was my best friend on the trail. He promised he would return and catch up with me so we could climb Katahdin together, just as we had taken our first steps together through the archway leading up to Springer Mountain. We hadn't hiked the whole way together, but every time I'd caught up to him, we picked right up where we left off. I think that is one of the true signs of a close friendship—it's not proximity to each other, how often you meet, or how long you've known each other, it's that ability to pick right up as if distance hasn't changed and time hasn't passed. But in that moment, seeing him go and knowing I wouldn't be running into him for some weeks—that made the journey just a little lonelier and me just a little sadder.

# 18

## BY MYSELF, NEVER ALONE

For the first time, I stumbled upon a bear far enough away that it either didn't know I was there or didn't care about my presence. That distance allowed me to take my time and watch without feeling I was in danger. For nearly twenty minutes, I sat there watching the bear wander about, eating berries. Eventually, it lowered onto its belly and shoved its head under a rock, looking for goodies, and I decided to move on.

I was alone after leaving my parents' home, and this was the longest stretch I was completely isolated from anyone on the trail, but I never felt lonely. It was like a walking meditation, a silent retreat that gave me the opportunity to be an observer in a way I couldn't be with others present.

The twenty-five-mile hike that day included Harriman State Park—a path of nostalgia as I'd hiked that wilderness and, in particular, the hike up to Island Pond so many times with various important people in my life. It felt like home was still with me.

Fingerboard Shelter gave me a comfortable camping spot that evening, with a dry, flat location for my tent. There was a tangible nervous vibe from the other hikers due to the high bear activity in the area. Unlike most, I considered that a plus. By this point in the trail, I'd become cautiously comfortable with the largest predator on the AT. I didn't distance my bear canister far away from my tent when I went to sleep at night; I kept it right next to me. If a wandering bear tried to batter its way to the food inside, I would have a front-row seat. It wasn't so much that I was brave or in control of my fears, but more that I had practiced letting go of the fear of what *could* happen. There is a real liberation in just living and accepting that what *will* happen…will happen.

The next morning, what could happen did happen, only it wasn't my bear canister, but another hiker's food bag. Other than the dawn's excitement, that day was highlighted by the constant presence of blueberries along the trail and my constant tendency to slow down because of them. Before this experience, I knew I liked blueberries, but I had no idea just how much of a distraction they could be. They were my roses, and I always stopped to smell them.

At the 1,400-mile mark, I came across two thru-hikers who introduced themselves as Funky Moon and DQ. They were hiking northbound as well and had been in Vernon a few days before me.

"You don't happen to be Scrambler?" one of them asked.

"I just so happen to be!" I replied excitedly and in some amount of disbelief. "How might you know me?"

"*Haha!* We met your mom," laughed the other hiker. "We were in the Acme in Vernon, and she walked up to us, said she smelled us from an aisle away and had to come say 'hi' because we reminded her of her son who was taking a short break at her house."

They were setting a decent pace, so the conversation quickly dispersed after that as we exchanged farewells. I'd gained another one of those unstoppable smiles that seemed to be happening more and more.

As I hiked through the southern part of New York state, I caught a glimpse of the New York City skyline in the distance. It was a symbol of my life left behind, and the sight of those buildings churned up deep feelings in me, just not the ones I would have guessed. Instead of resentment or bitterness or loss, I was filled with gratitude for everything that former life had taught me. I had spent four of those ten years working in the pharmaceutical advertising industry in the city, and I could see now that it was an important part of my journey. Its greatest contribution to who I was becoming was in showing me what I didn't want in life and had pushed me to a place where I was broken enough to accept that. Even though I felt I'd left that life far behind, I knew the greatest challenge was still ahead—would I continue to choose my heart…or default back to old habits?

I stopped in at Tony's Deli near Pawling, a New York staple on the trail, not only for their delicious hot food but also for their kind treatment and hospitality toward thru-hikers, offering up their property for tent-camping. I stopped at the Dover Oak, reported to be the largest tree on the entire Appalachian Trail. At over three hundred years old with more than a twenty-foot circumference, when I gave it a hug goodbye, I was barely able to get my arms around one portion of its massive trunk.

Leaving the next morning, I was glad I'd made my memory of the New York leg of my hike a simple and pleasant one. New

York would always hold a special place in my heart. Venturing into Connecticut that day meant I'd completed nine states with five more to go. That wasn't the only milestone of Day Eighty-five. I'd come to the official two-thirds mark of the trail. I was now over 66% of the way to Katahdin. Heading deeper into Connecticut, I let my mindset lapse due to all the claims that this was a "flat" state. I soon was faced by a series of PUDs (pointless ups and downs) that lasted for two full days and reinforced the truth that no state on the Appalachian Trail is *flat*.

That second day in Connecticut brought me to another major milestone—the 1,500-mile mark and the arrival at Maria McCabe's home in Salisbury. Maria is an elderly woman who has been opening up her home to thru-hikers for years and is often referred to as the "nicest woman on the trail". Reviews in various trail guides describe her place as "staying at your grandma's house." These claims were not exaggerated. This wonderful woman welcomed me into her home, let me use her shower, and drove me to a laundromat where I washed my clothes and was able to secure a warm meal. That is not to mention her warmth and openness, making me feel like I had somehow wandered back to my family home in New Jersey.

After a breakfast of over-easy eggs the next morning, I decided to adopt a more restful pace and hike only twelve miles that day. I'm glad I did. I was near the top of Bear Mountain, and I could hear two birds making loud noises. Bird sounds happen a thousand times on the trail and had never caused me to look, but this morning, I looked back over my shoulder. There, perched on a branch just off the trail, having nothing to do with the noisy birds that had drawn my attention, was a small baby owl staring back at me. Its gaze seemed curious, not fearful, almost like a human baby. The small creature blinked long at me, and I returned a long blink back. We repeated this communication a few more times. Not wanting to trespass too long on this animal's time and space or draw the agitation of an unseen parent, I set off again, thinking if I had been hiking my usual pace, I never would have shared that moment with the baby owl. The trail continued to remind me that life really was about pacing oneself, not racing to the finish line. The destination was important, and I eagerly looked forward to achieving my goal, but the time I had now was for the journey.

The next day, I stopped into an antique store just off the trail, not to browse their excellent collection of doorknobs and stained glass, but because they held a small fridge containing something I had consumed more in the past eighty-eight days than at any other point in my life. Before the trail, I'd never really craved soda. It just wasn't a part of my healthy life. But on the trail, there were miles where the specific desire for that sweet, cold, carbonated beverage was greater than any other craving. I wanted it...*all the time*. And I got it.

That night at camp, I enjoyed the rest of my soda—which I'd saved for a relaxing evening—while listening to stories from another northbound hiker. These included the tale of a man bitten by a rabid skunk and the regaling of another fellow who had blown his hand off trying to start a campfire with gunpowder. I was reminded of these stories later off-trail when I met a man who is now a friend of mine. He told me his AT story, a story that was one day long. He took a wrong step coming down from Springer Mountain in Georgia and tore his MCL. That was the start and end of his time on the trail. I lay there that night grateful for the safe and catastrophe-free hike I'd had.

The next day I was visited by Nick and Kate, two friends I'd made during my time working in NYC. In true trail angel fashion, they brought with them an Italian sub (my favorite) and homemade chocolate chip cookies. It was a nice taste of life off the trail, but not so nice as Nick and Kate driving three hours to see me, then hiking with me for four hours. Me being the big bad thru-hiker, I naturally took the lead but had forgotten something important. I turned around at one point and found both of my friends holding their noses in the wake of my trail stench. We adjusted our positions in line. We ended our jaunt together at a beautiful pond about fifteen miles into my day and took a couple hours to rest and catch up, just enjoying each other's company, me sitting downwind.

After Nick and Kate's departure, I timed the last leg of the day to end not far from Dalton, Mass, a marquee location for any thru-hiker. Not only does Dalton sport a charming downtown with a small assortment of eateries, but it's also the home of Tom Levardi, one of the prominent trail angel "celebrities," much like Maria McCabe.

Mr. Levardi's home is conveniently located right off the main drag through town. He offers up his substantial yard for thru-hikers to set up camp. In addition, he provides breakfast for all who come. I stopped in for a short while, not intending to overnight. Even though I wasn't making his yard my stay, Tom still offered me coffee and doughnuts, which I happily accepted.

At the local Juice and Java, drinking my freshly pressed super greens, I was struck by just how hiker-friendly the town was. I had been greeted by only smiles and conversation in Dalton. It made me think about this concept, being "hiker-friendly," the simple act of being kind to the "others" of society. When imagining these others, I pictured a homeless man and immediately wondered why that was my first thought. I had lived in enough places to know that "other" was a changing definition, tied to what was "normal" from one region to the next—a different lifestyle, background, or set of beliefs. But it didn't really matter what "other" meant. No matter what a person's life looked like, no matter where it had begun or what had colored its days, I could choose to be kind. How different my trail experience would have been had so many not treated me with acceptance and kindness, a simple free act, one that so many of us withhold.

# 19

## ONE KIND ACT

After prying myself from the warm embrace of Dalton, I hiked several more miles that evening, taking on the tallest mountain in Massachusetts, Mount Greylock. On the hike up that slope, I met two hikers, Rocket and Wild Turkey. But these weren't just ordinary hikers. This particular day, they were there with the intention of being trail angels, handing out ice cream packed in a cooler filled with dry ice. I gladly accepted a frozen Twix to add a little extra fuel for my next big day. I had planned to hike twenty miles or more, which would carry me across the border into Vermont. Life on the trail often has other plans.

After a short side-trail and breathtaking view from a peak that morning, I returned to the main trail, feeling rejuvenated. About a mile later, I was greeted by familiar faces. Speedo and Lieutenant Dan were two fellow thru-hikers I'd met briefly way down south in Virginia but hadn't seen since. They were joined by someone new, a tall, lanky guy who would soon introduce himself as SoS (Swag of Switzerland) in a thick Swiss accent.

"Hey Scrambler," Speedo called out in his own Aussie accent as they approached, "Why you headin' south?"

I cocked my head to the side. "Why are you guys heading south?" I shot back, half-joking, half-not understanding the joke.

SoS simply looked up at the morning sun, low in the sky to their right, also known as East.

I spun around, reorienting myself to the sun and the shadows, pointing at various things like I was attempting to solve a murder mystery. After a moment, my head dropped in embarrassing acceptance.

"No worries," Speedo chuckled. "We'll set you right."

With a mix of laughter and friendly ribbing, we set off together, *north* towards Vermont, our steps lightened by the camaraderie and often humbling humor of the trail. The joking continued at every opportunity until we found ourselves at the nearest main road, at which I learned my three new hiking mates had already made up their minds that this was to be for them a nearo day for rest and resupply in Williamstown, Massachusetts. I decided one more day of letting my aching limbs and feet recuperate would not be a terrible thing.

A short distance down the road, we came to a small shopping plaza with a Stop 'n Shop grocery store. The blast of air conditioning as we walked through the automatic doors was a welcome relief from the thick summer heat. We stocked up on supplies and continued until we found a shaded spot to sit and wait for the local Papa John's pizza to open.

While sitting, a few other thru-hikers wandered up to the Stop 'n Shop and introduced themselves. Still glowing from the frozen Twix the day before, I felt a sudden inspiration and disappeared back into the store and returned with a box of fresh donuts to share, hoping to return a little trail magic for the magic I'd received. This kind of impulse was so rare in my former life, and when the opportunity presented itself, I was usually "too busy" to act.

Eyes widened and hands reached for the sugary treats in gratifying displays of pure joy.

"You didn't have to do this!" Lieutenant Dan said, his mouth decorated with chocolate frosting.

"I know," I replied with a smile. "I just wanted to."

When Papa John's finally opened, we were pleasantly surprised to learn our meal would be 50% off, just for being thru-hikers. Lieutenant Dan informed me the owner was a former thru-hiker himself and understood the hiker-hunger affliction.

After our pizza feast, we found our way to the Maple Terrace Motel, our weary bodies grateful for a hot shower and soft bed. That night, Speedo, Lieutenant Dan, and I caught up with each other's journeys past Virginia, and though I had only hiked with Speedo briefly and only met Lieutenant Dan while staying at the Woods Hole Hostel, there was no awkwardness at our regroup. It was an instant belonging.

"Anyone up for a swim?" SoS suggested. Within minutes, the four of us were enjoying the luxury of weightlessness that can only be experienced after spending so many days hauling heavy packs up and down steep inclines.

The following morning, we filled our stomachs with a hearty breakfast at a small diner in town before venturing back up to the trail toward the state line.

"Three states left," I murmured to myself as we crossed into Vermont, something I could never have imagined saying before that experience as we passed the 1,600-mile mark of the Appalachian Trail. The end may have been a little less than six-hundred miles away, but it felt more tangible than it ever had before. For the first time, I allowed myself to believe I could actually conquer this incredible journey.

Our first full day in Vermont was a challenging twenty-eight-mile hike through some of the most picturesque landscapes I had ever seen. As we climbed higher, the mixed woods gradually gave way to towering pine forests. The scent of fresh pine needles filled my lungs, reinvigorating me with each breath.

"Guys, check this out!" Speedo called from ahead, drawing our attention to one of the fire towers perched atop an impressive peak. We scrambled up the steps, our legs burning with the effort. Reaching the top, we were rewarded with a breathtaking panorama of deep green foothills, stretching out as far as the eye could see. The vibrant foliage of Vermont seemed to swallow us into it, encapsulating the full essence of the "Green Mountain State" moniker the state boasted.

After some time back on the trail, the sound of steps ahead caused me to look up and pause in my tracks. I saw a family of three making their way toward us. They looked like any other thru-hikers we'd encountered on the AT, fitted out with well-appointed packs and gear, nothing unordinary until I saw the smallest member of their group—a little girl walking slowly beside her mother, barely tall enough to see over the tall grasses lining the trail.

"Hi there!" the child's mom greeted us warmly as they drew near. "I'm Kanga. This is my husband, Sherpa. And this is Roo," she turned to her daughter and lovingly held up the child's arm. "You might know her on social media as "Ellie on the AT.""

"Nice to meet you," I replied, smiling down at the wide-eyed toddler who stared back up at me with as much apparent curiosity. "I'm Scrambler, and these are my friends Lieutenant Dan, Speedo, and SoS."

"Ellie here has been hiking the AT with us since she was twelve months old," Sherpa explained, his voice full of pride. "Haven't you, Ellie?"

She babbled something as though she had completely understood her father's question and with complete faith that we comprehended her response.

"We started at McAfee Knob," he continued, "and hiked south to Springer Mountain, Georgia. Now we're heading down from Katahdin back to McAfee Knob to finish up."

"Wow! That's quite a feat!" I beamed toward their daughter.

Ellie just gazed at me with her big, curious eyes, taking in every detail of my appearance.

As we continued to chat, I felt a genuine wonder toward Kanga and Sherpa and an admiration for doing something I wasn't sure I could have done in their place. The logistics alone of bringing a toddler on a thru-hike, let alone the fears a parent must feel, yet here they were, immersing their child in the beauty of nature and teaching her the importance of following one's passions. She might not remember it when she grew up, but they'll have every picture to show her what she accomplished at such a young age. What a gift—what a thing to be able to say to your child later when they are struggling.

"Honey, I know it's tough, but remember, you hiked the entire Appalachian Trail before you were two years old."

"I'm amazed," I said out loud before realizing I was saying it.

Kanga let out a gentle laugh. "Yeah, she's our little trail angel. She reminds us each day why we're out here."

I thought about Ellie and her parents long after we had parted ways. I reflected on my own journey on the Appalachian Trail, how it had changed me for the better and how it might have served me so well to have experienced it early in life. Even as an adult in my thirties, the AT had taught me so much about myself, about resilience, and staying true to who I am. It had taught me to notice the little things. It had taught me gratitude. I wondered again how I might bring that to people who didn't have this experience, to give back what I had gained. I was certain I could; I just had to figure out how.

The sun had dipped below the horizon, casting a fiery glow across the sky as we made our way into Manchester.

"Man, I'm starving," Lieutenant Dan said, his stomach audibly growling in agreement with the rest of ours.

"Manchester House of Pizza is supposed to be great," SoS chimed in, that is if you guys aren't tired of pizza yet.

"Hi," I said, reaching out a hand to SoS. "I don't know if we've met. I'm Ryan, and I'm a pizza-holic."

It was a quick stop in a charming town, and after devouring several slices, we found ourselves hitchhiking back to the trail on a local public bus.

As the days continued, I wished more than once that bus would swoop through and carry me to my next destination. The beauty of Vermont continued to unfold before us—one breathtaking peak after another. But as much as I reveled in the stunning landscape, I couldn't ignore the growing ache in my feet and knees. It was a deep, relentless pain that refused to subside no matter how much I rested or massaged.

As we neared the 1,700-mile mark of our journey, the weight of my pack seemed to grow with each step. Despite the pain, I continued the same pace I'd maintained for the last nearly one-hundred days. There were many things buoying my performance—the confidence I'd gained on the trail, my desire to complete it, and perhaps more than anything, the fact that there was always something to look forward to each day, something to keep me wandering, sometimes, a destination. This night, it was a treat for me and my companions.

"I've got a special gift for us tonight," I said with a grin as the sun began to dip. "An old colleague is treating us to a stay at the Inn at Long Trail." I held up the gift card I'd been given as a parting gift, good for a one-night stay for me and whoever was with me. "Wait," I said, as the thanks began pouring in. "That's not all... We're also having dinner tonight with another friend. His name is Sujay. He and his wife, Teresa, are joining us."

As we arrived at the inn, Sujay and Teresa were waiting for us with warm smiles. We exchanged hugs and launched into a night filled with laughter, good food, and reminiscing. An Irish band plied us with lively tunes, and when it came time to pay for our meal, the server informed us that someone had already covered our bill. I looked around, wondering who the generous stranger was, but they remained anonymous. Later that night, we learned there was a "celebrity" trail angel named Miss Janet at the restaurant. She hadn't even introduced herself, but in a moment of pure kindness that continued to surprise me, even though I had experienced many by then, she paid for our food in silence and left us to enjoy the company we had arrived with. At least, we believed it was her. Miss Janet, if it was you, I never had a chance to thank you. Thank you.

The next day, while resupplying in Rutland, I was visited by Josh, a childhood friend. In true Josh fashion, he gifted me a bottle of pure Vermont maple syrup with instructions to take a swig when I needed a little sugar rush. The bottle would be emptied before I even left the state.

Hartford, Vermont, was next on the map, the home of a locally well-known trail angel named Linda. As we approached her thru-hiker barn, the famous giant AT symbol greeted us from the front. Before we could knock on the door, a bark echoed through the air. Linda's dog, Tucker, bounded towards us, wagging his tail furiously. For all his noise, he was as gentle as a lamb.

"Welcome, hikers!" Linda called out with a smile. "My home is your home."

"Thank you so much," I responded, stepping into the cozy barn.

We settled in for the night, and each of us shared stories of the incredible kindness and support we had experienced on the trail. The evening sun cast golden rays across the barnwood as Linda shared her own story with us. For over two decades, she had been opening her doors to weary hikers, providing respite and nourishment without asking for a single cent. I was humbled by her generosity, and my mind drifted once more to how I could carry this mentality forward from the trail.

That evening, nestled in the cozy confines of Linda's barn, I received a message from BAMF. My eyes scanned the words on my phone, the weight of their meaning settling heavy within my chest and casting a shadow over the events of the day. BAMF's journey was over. He had pressing matters to attend to with work and would be flying directly home from the wedding in Madagascar.

As the sun dipped below the horizon, I couldn't help but feel the loss. Despite the beauty of this journey, this felt akin to losing a member of my trail family, a void that could not easily be filled.

# 20

## UNDER THE MIST, ABOVE THE WORLD

A true angel of the trail, Linda had already begun breakfast before we stirred the following morning. The smell of coffee, muffins, eggs, and sausage was my alarm clock, and my stomach rumbled, waking me up to the world. As I sipped my coffee, the warmth spreading through my body was a soothing prelude to the roaring chorus that lay ahead.

"Gettin' ready for the 'Whites', eh?" Linda asked, flipping an egg.

I nodded, both excited and nervous for what was to come. Speedo joined me at the table, his eyes lighting up at the meal before us.

"Thanks, Linda," he said, digging in with gusto. "This is just what we needed."

"You'll need more than that to take on the Whites," said Linda, and we all knew she was referring to the kind of sustenance we couldn't put in our stomachs. From what we had heard, we would need a fierce resolve.

As we ate, we chatted about our upcoming challenges and the infamous Whites awaiting us in New Hampshire. Thoughts of those mountains had been looming for some time. But first, we had to cross the state line at the Connecticut River. This official entry into the "Granite State" seemed like a milestone worth celebrating, and I felt a renewed sense of determination course through me.

"Alright, let's go." I stood resolute, hoisting my pack onto my shoulders almost as if going to war. We bid Linda farewell and fueled by food and gratitude, continued on our journey.

The morning hike was pleasant, the forest floor damp beneath our boots, the scent of pine needles mingling with the earthy aroma of the moss-laden woods. Not far into that day, we encountered some unexpected trail magic from a fellow thru-hiker named Short and Sweet. She handed us each a sizable portion of chocolate chip banana bread, her smile wide and infectious.

"Good luck in the Whites, y'all!" she called out as we continued on our way. She had stopped just long enough to share and move on.

Not long after, we stumbled upon Dan and Whit's General Store, directly off the trail, where they were giving away left-over breakfast sandwiches to thru-hikers. Speedo and I eagerly accepted the proffered sandwiches knowing there was no amount of food our hiker hunger couldn't make short work of. It seemed as if the universe knew what awaited us.

With full bellies, we approached the Connecticut River, the shimmering water marking the border between Vermont and New Hampshire. We paused for a moment, silently taking in the significance of crossing this threshold.

"Here we come, White Mountains," I whispered as we moved forward, feeling both the weight of the challenge ahead and the exhilaration of moving ever closer to our goal.

The small town of Hanover welcomed us with open arms, its streets buzzing with the energy of Dartmouth College students and locals alike. Speedo and I meandered through the town's center, feeling the weight of our backpacks lighten as we embraced this respite from the trail.

"Check this out," Speedo said, pointing to a sign in the window of Romunto's Pizzeria. "Free slice of pizza for thru-hikers!"

"Would be a crime to pass up," I replied, my mouth already watering.

Inside, friendly staff greeted us with smiles and handed out warm slices of pizza. We devoured them gratefully. Hanover wasn't done caring for us, though. Our next stop was Lou's, where free donuts awaited. As we indulged in these unexpected treats, I couldn't help but wonder if the vibrant student population of Hanover played a role in fostering such a hiker-friendly atmosphere.

While enjoying the bounty of Hanover, Speedo and I met up with Chris, a man whose life had been deeply affected by cystic fibrosis. He had lost his brother to the disease and lived with it himself. The moment we began speaking, I felt an instant connection.

"CF has taught me to appreciate every breath I take," he told us during our meeting, his eyes filled with both sorrow and the resilience that came with surviving it. "Live life to the fullest, despite the challenges."

I was continually amazed by the optimism of those who suffered and survived, especially those who had experienced the loss CF could bring. I thought back to my time spent with each of those touched by CF, how their stories of resilience had been so like Chris'. Sitting down with Chris and listening to his experiences, I felt even more committed to living my life in a way that uplifted others and shared the best parts of myself with them.

"Your strength is truly inspiring," I told him, my heart swelling with gratitude for the encounter. "Thank you for sharing your story with us."

"Thank you for listening," he replied. "It means the world."

Speedo and I eventually said our goodbyes to Chris and Hanover, and again I felt a weight, only this was one I wanted to carry—a responsibility to take every bit of growth from the trail and mold it into a life of service, to bring shared experiences and instill hope and encouragement in those enduring hardships.

"Are you okay?" Speedo asked.

"Yeah," I answered, smiling through the tears that threatened to fall. "Just feeling really grateful."

Day 100 would soon arrive—a day I'd been looking forward to, that I'd imagined waking up to with all the glory of the experiences that had come before and the hope of what lay ahead. The morning had other plans.

"*Beep!...Beep!...Beep!...*" Speedo's alarm clock shattered my dreamy haze, jolting me awake with a thud back to reality. The sun hadn't even begun to grace the sky.

"Speedooooooo…" I moaned, "why are you setting an alarm?"

"Sorry, man," Speedo muttered as he fumbled with his phone. "I just... I want to be done, man. I want to get to Katahdin and get back home, you know?"

I sighed, fighting my gut reaction of annoyance. Staring at the tent ceiling, I took a moment to consider his words. I understood Speedo's longing—the familiar comforts of home, the physical relief—but I couldn't go there with him. I couldn't succumb to the eagerness to rush through the final stretch of our journey. I didn't want that. I contemplated what I did want out of the remaining days ahead. It was simple and clear for me. I wanted to savor every moment, take in every breathtaking view, cherish every surprise offered.

I valued the camaraderie and shared experience so much with Speedo and every other hiker I'd met along the way. But the last thing I wanted was for the last few weeks on the trail to feel like just another job to wake up for, complete, then fall asleep. I promised to check in with myself each day and make sure I was continuing to hike my own hike at my own pace, and if that ever wasn't true, I would make an adjustment. Day one hundred was going to be a good day, I determined.

My mind buzzed with a mix of excitement and nervousness as we broke camp. As we hiked the two miles to the sign that said, "Welcome to the Whites," I tried to focus on the present moment, though that was difficult knowing that what lay just ahead were the infamous peaks.

"Hey guys, look!" Speedo called out, pointing ahead. Just off the trail was a makeshift workstation complete with a stove, pots, pans, and an assortment of ingredients. The famous "Omelet Guy" stood behind the counter, grinning from ear to ear.

"Morning, thru-hikers!" he greeted us warmly. "How many eggs in your omelets this morning?"

"How many can we have?" I asked, half-joking.

"As many as you want," he replied, no joke whatsoever in his expression.

"Seriously?"

"Seriously," he replied with a wink. "The record is twenty-four, but I don't recommend trying to beat it."

"I'll take your advice. Five will do for me," I said, taking a seat on a nearby log, watching in awe as Omelet Guy whipped up fluffy, golden masterpieces before our eyes.

"Here you go," he said, placing the steaming plate in front of me. "Enjoy!"

I did, and it was exactly what I needed mentally and physically.

The initial ascent up Mount Moosilauke was every bit as difficult as people made it out to be. My legs burned with each step, but the thought of reaching the peak kept me going. As we climbed higher, I found myself breathing harder, the thinning air challenging my pace.

*Keep pushing*, I thought, focusing on the rhythm of my breath.

As we emerged above the tree line, we paused to take in the panorama unfolding before us—the many peaks of White Mountain National Forest stretching out like a giant green and gray tapestry, where dark pines stopped at craggy slopes.

"Wow," I whispered, my fatigue momentarily forgotten.

"Yeah," returned Speedo. "Just... Yeah."

With newfound determination, we pushed onward, grinding our way up the final few hundred feet to the summit. We celebrated with a slow lunch and sat there enjoying the view and relishing the shared cathartic experience.

"Does it get any better than this, do you think?" I asked both the group and myself.

"I'm not sure it does," replied SoS.

The next morning, my body ached as I woke up, the sun filtering through the window of The Notch Hostel, casting a warm glow over the bunk beds and piles of gear strewn about. But there was less sting in the ache—for the first time since New Jersey, I was taking a zero day, and my body seemed aware of the decision. I rose early, having decided the night before that I would take on the role of breakfast trail angel.

"Hey," I called out to my fellow hikers as I wandered into the common area, "who's up for some pancakes?"

The response was enthusiastic, and soon we were all gathered around the kitchen as I flipped pancakes on the griddle. It had been ages since I'd enjoyed a leisurely morning like this, and it felt like a luxury to indulge in the simple pleasure of cooking for friends.

After breakfast, we sprawled out across the hostel, some reading, others napping, and a small group of us locked in a fierce game of Uno.

As evening fell, I found myself sitting on the porch, watching the sun set over the mountains we'd conquered yesterday. Bookie, the woman who ran The Notch Hostel and who had picked us up from the trail the evening before, approached me, her eyes lighting up with curiosity.

"So, Scrambler, I heard you mention to the others that you are hiking for cystic fibrosis."

I nodded. "Yeah, that's me."

"That's really incredible," she said. "I'm working on a publication called 'People of the Whites.' I actually looked up your story on Instagram, 'Breathtaking Journey.' Do you mind if I ask you some questions?"

"Oh...sure," I replied, half-embarrassed to know someone was actually following my story but more surprised.

Bookie pulled out a small recorder and began asking me about my hike, my motivations, and how I hoped to make an impact by dedicating my journey to cystic fibrosis awareness.

I don't remember much of what I said, only that by the end, I felt a little less like an imposter for carrying the flag I'd had with me all this way to raise cystic fibrosis awareness. By that point, it shouldn't have surprised me that there were people like Bookie wanting to cast such a positive light on what we were all doing. I think it's hard to leave behind that skepticism when you've used it all your life as a protection and as a reflection of your own motivations, making you doubt others.

"Good luck on the rest of your journey," Bookie said, shaking my hand before heading inside. "Keep making a difference."

"Thanks," I replied. "I hope to."

The morning after staying at The Notch Hostel, we embarked on a challenging stretch of the trail. Speedo was eager to push us hard, and while I agreed to continue with him, my body still ached from the days spent traversing the Whites. Our pace quickened as the trees blurred past us, their shadows dancing around like ghosts in the undergrowth. I clenched my teeth and forced myself to keep up, beads of sweat forming on my brow. As much as I wanted to share Speedo's enthusiasm for getting to the end, my heart wasn't entirely in it. The mountains seemed to loom larger with each quickly passing mile. I couldn't help but begin to feel I was missing out on the experience of them. That fear was confirmed later that day.

As we made camp at Liberty Springs Campground that evening, we met a group of hikers who had seen a moose on the trail earlier in the day. My eyes widened at the news, a pang of disappointment settling in my chest.

"Ah man, I can't believe we missed it," I muttered to Speedo, trying to hide my frustration. "That would have been something to see."

"Hey, there's always next time," he replied, attempting to cheer me up. I knew logically it didn't matter how fast or slow I had hiked that day, I still might not have seen the moose, but in my heart, I couldn't stifle the feeling that our hurried pace had cost us the opportunity. Another notch was carved in a growing belt of tension between me and the pace we were setting.

The following day, however, my spirits began to rise as we approached the famed Franconia Ridge. I'd been looking forward to this portion of the hike for months, having read about its breathtaking vistas in every trail guide I'd come across. Despite the pace and lingering ache in my muscles, I felt renewed excitement as we navigated the rocky terrain leading up to the ridge.

We camped close to the top that night, carefully planning our stop to savor the anticipation and give us a short hike up the fabled ridge the following morning. We slept under the stars, and during the night, those stars disappeared.

The morning greeted us with a fog so dense, it was as if the world beyond our camp had ceased to exist. I shivered despite the many layers I wore, my breath visible against the gray curtain. We ate a quick breakfast and broke camp, eager and hopeful that the many peaks of Franconia Ridge would lie above the shroud.

"Man, it's cold," Speedo said as we began our ascent, his hands tucked into the pockets of his jacket. "Feels like nature's playing a cruel joke on us."

"Hopefully it clears up," I said, trying to muster some optimism, as much for myself as the others. As we climbed higher, the wind picked up, biting at our exposed skin with icy teeth, despite being mid-summer.

Each step brought us closer to the famed ridge, but the fog showed no signs of lifting. Our footsteps fell heavy on the rocky trail, muffled by the thick blanket. It felt as though we were moving through a dream, the world around us existing only in lighter and darker shades of gray and the muted deep greens of the evergreen forest cloaked in the misty shroud.

"Can you see anything?" I asked Speedo during a brief pause. "Anything at all?"

"Nothing," he replied.

That morning, we summited Little Haystack, Lincoln, Lafayette, and Garfield mountains, all hidden from our eager gazes. Each point felt like a triumph, not only physically over the steep ascents but in our minds climbing over the disappointment of how little of the heralded terrain we could actually see. By the time we stopped for lunch, I feared the entirety of my Franconia Ridge experience would be marred.

I spent lunch only half-participating in the conversation around me. The other half of my focus was spent trying to quell my disappointment. I tried reminding myself of the many previous lessons of the trail, that one "can't turn off the rain" and that my true reasons for embarking on this journey had nothing to do with seeing a particular view but to change the one within. After a while, I began to feel an easing of the dispirit and a return to gratitude for the totality of the experience, though I can admit to myself now, I would have traded it in that moment for a few minutes of clear hiking.

We finished our lunch and strode down from the peak of Garfield Mountain, and no sooner had we entered the tree line, as if in response to my new resolve, the trail gods began to lift the fog around us. The world around us came into focus: rugged peaks giving way to vast, sweeping valleys, their slopes carpeted in green with dense white cloud cover rolling away. We were treated to vista after breathtaking vista, culminating in a 360-degree view from South Twin Mountain that left me speechless.

"Wow," Speedo whispered, echoing my thoughts. "Now this...this is why we're out here."

I smiled, my heart swelling with appreciation for the beauty that surrounded us. We had come to find mountains, and there found the wild in our hearts.

The remainder of that day was a symphony of breathtaking views and invigorating climbs. We hiked Mounts Guyot, Zeacliff, and Zealand, their peaks offering generous rewards for our efforts. The doldrums of the morning had long since been forgotten, replaced by the exhilaration of pushing ourselves to new heights and the views from them.

As twilight enveloped the mountains, we arrived at Zealand Falls Hut. Nestled in a verdant valley below the summit of Zealand Mountain, the hut was a welcome oasis for weary hikers. Its wooden beams and cozy interior offered a taste of home, while its expansive windows framed the rugged landscape that had become our playground.

Zealand was the first of the AMC Huts as hikers called them, a string of eight accommodations operated by the Appalachian Mountain Club. AMC Huts are one of the most unique experiences on the AT, not only because of the unsurpassed amenities but because of the deal the owners had worked out with thru-hikers. We help out around the hut, and they let us sleep there and eat the leftovers from dinner.

That night, we feasted on the remnants of a hearty meal—savory stews, crusty bread, and tender vegetables—until our bellies were full and our spirits restored. In exchange, we washed dishes, swept floors, and assisted with various chores around the hut. It was a small price to pay.

The following days found us navigating the spectacular vistas of Crawford Notch and the Presidential Range, each summit revealing new panoramas. We stayed at Lakes of the Clouds Hut, another one of the AMC Huts, offering stunning views from an elevation of 5,050 feet within the saddle between Mt. Washington and Mt. Monroe. Our bodies ached from the relentless climbs, but our souls soared in the presence of such beauty. The following morning, we were enlisted to carry rolls of toilet paper to the last of the Appalachian Mountain Club huts we would see, Madison Springs. They were so happy at our arrival with much-needed provisions, they offered us free bowls of soup and leftover blueberry bread. From there, our trek brought us to Pinkham Notch, where we stealth camped in a dirt parking lot beside an idle tractor. It was no AMC Hut, but a testament to the adaptability hiking the AT sometimes required.

The next day began with an all-you-can-eat breakfast buffet at the Pinkham Notch Visitor Center. As I savored each delicious bite, I marveled at the ever-changing weaving of experiences along the trail, each unique and memorable in its own way. But while my adventurous spirit was being refilled anew each day, it had been about a week since my body was no longer recovering the way it had after the first several days on the trail.

As we continued, the days began to shorten, not due to the length of time the sun was in the sky but because of the duration of miles my body could keep up with my desire. I hurt with every step from my feet to my head. Hiking the Appalachian Trail for 107 days had demanded a physical toll from me, and the toll was only increasing.

I found my thoughts drifting towards Katahdin in a way I had not yet experienced. It was bordering on obsessive. Usually, I would have steered my focus away from the end prize and returned them to the present moment, but I figured I was close enough that the distance no longer felt daunting, and a little distraction from the pain was welcome. I wondered if this is what Speedo had been experiencing those several days before when I grumbled about his alarm clock.

As I pressed onward, my mind wrestled with conflicting emotions. On one hand, I longed for the comfort of home and the familiar faces I'd left behind. On the other hand, a growing sense of loss that this once-in-a-lifetime experience was drawing to a close.

# 21

## NOTCH

The sun had just breached the horizon when I awoke, my breath visible in the crisp morning air. The scent of dewy grass filled my nose as I emerged from my tent, eager for the day ahead. SoS, Speedo, and I were only a short hike away from the road leading into Gorham, NH, and we were looking forward to a hot breakfast to pair with our much-needed resupply in town.

After packing our things, we made our way to the road and managed a hitch from a friendly local into town. He gave us his recommendation for breakfast, and it didn't disappoint. The smell of bacon and fresh coffee enveloped us as we entered the bustling diner. We devoured our breakfast like three starved animals, the warmth spreading through our cold bodies.

Once our hunger was appeased, and we had become human again, we decided to explore the quaint little town of Gorham before resupplying for the next stretch of days. As we ambled down one of the streets, we heard distant shouting but couldn't quite make out the words. The noise seemed to be coming from a yellow school bus, and it was barreling toward us. We stopped and watched as it drew closer. It never slowed. As the bus flew by, its captain stuck his head out the driver-side window and yelled, "HikerYearbook.com!"

Odie! I recognized him instantly. A well-known past thru-hiker, Odie ran HikerYearbook.com, driving the length of the trail each year in his big yellow bus, documenting AT hikers' stories and experiences. He was somewhat famous in hiking circles, and I had secretly hoped to meet him during my trek, mainly because of his role in keeping the trail community close. Being shouted at by him, unfortunately, was as close as I ever got.

We stocked up on supplies at Walmart and grabbed a quick lunch at the White Mountain Cafe before hitching back to the trail, energized by our brush with fame. The afternoon hike out of Gorham was tough, but we pushed through, covering eleven miles and crossing the 1,900-mile mark, just four miles from Maine's border.

That night, as I lay in my tent, my mind wandered to Katahdin. I loved this life, but I couldn't stop myself from imagining what it would be like to wake up in a bed. That wasn't what I truly wanted; I knew that, not yet. It was only the parts of me that ached and shivered and burned that wanted relief.

I actively shifted my thoughts to the beauty of the wilderness surrounding me. SoS had mentioned earlier that he had heard there was a moose that frequented this location because of a nearby pond, and I allowed my mind to be filled with anticipation at the possibility of seeing it the next morning as I drifted off to sleep.

The next morning, I awoke to the patter of raindrops on my tent, a sign of things to come. Although we had been prepared for wet weather, I wasn't prepared for the icy cold that accompanied it. As SoS and I stepped out of our tents, shivering under our rain gear, we exchanged glances, acknowledging the miserable conditions. Then we gritted our teeth and stepped onto the winding trail, the rich forest greens muted by the relentless downpour.

The rain drenched our clothes and drained our energy. My mind wandered back to the warmth of the White Mountain Cafe, and I tried to hold onto that memory to keep me going. Focusing on the adventure proved challenging. I found myself fighting the desire to escape this discomfort while dealing with the reality that there was no way around it, only through.

The path was slippery to begin with and became only more treacherous with each passing mile of slick rocks and thick mud. Despite my best effort at careful navigation, I lost my footing that morning for the second time on the trail. The first fall, back in Virginia, had been nothing more than a bruised ego and a sore butt. This time, however, I went careening over the side of the trail, tumbling and sliding down about thirty feet.

"Are you okay?" SoS shouted, rushing to the edge of the path and peering down at me.

By some miracle, I had landed in a patch of moss so thick it swallowed my arm up to my shoulder and had cushioned the rest of me. The natural landing pad had saved me from what would have almost certainly been serious injury. I found myself unscathed, albeit shaken and a little ego-bruised.

"Yeah…I'm alright," I reassured him, my voice trembling with adrenaline.

"Be careful coming back up," he cautioned, extending a hand.

As we resumed our hike, I was acutely aware of the danger we both faced and suddenly found it much easier to focus past the difficult and onto the task at hand.

We crossed the border into Maine that day. Even though we were soaked through to our skin and freezing cold, we stuck around long enough to capture a photo with the final state line crossing sign. The milestone filled me with both excitement and apprehension. The final state on my Appalachian Trail journey lay before me, a testament to how far I'd come and a reminder of the challenges that still awaited. With the fall fresh in my mind, I knew we needed to regroup and rest up for the notorious Mahoosuc Notch.

"Let's call it a day," I suggested. "We've got a tough stretch ahead of us. We need to be at our best."

"Sounds like a plan," replied SoS, his voice steady but carrying a hint of relief.

Even Speedo agreed that calling it a day was the smartest decision.

We made it to a shelter for the night, nestled among towering pines. As I unpacked my gear, SoS pulled out a deck of cards, challenging me to a few rounds of Golf. We played and conversed, enjoying the rare opportunity to catch our breath on the trail and just enjoy each other's company. Afterward, we feasted on my legendary trail mashed potatoes which always hit the spot. Despite the long days of hiking, it was these moments that reminded me—and in some ways taught me—why I had chosen this journey, that return to deep human connection found far out in the woods.

We savored the last bites of our humble feast, and I retreated into the sanctuary of my sleeping bag, a cocoon of nylon and mesh that had become my home over these past months. I lay there listening to the gentle rustle of leaves and the distant call of a loon, feeling the cold wind on my face. Despite the chill, a warmth spread within me. We had reached Maine, the final state on our Appalachian Trail journey.

So many who begin this adventure never get to experience the wild beauty of this farthest corner of the trail. The thought of my recent fall still haunted me; how easily it could have been the end, and not just the hike. The weather had played its part, but I had too. I closed my eyes, taking a deep breath of the crisp air that filled the shelter, and made a promise to myself: slow down, appreciate each little moment.

"Hey…" SoS whispered, gently shaking me awake the next morning. "Looks like we've got company."

Blinking away the haze of slumber, Speedo was already gazing out of the shelter. I followed his eyes to find a dog sitting patiently near our campsite, as though its master had brought it there, commanded it to "stay," and left. A GPS collar with a small tag indicated this was someone's pet. Its soulful eyes seemed to plead with us, as if asking for help.

"Maybe it'll be gone by the time we're ready to leave," I suggested, my voice still thick with sleep. My groggy mind reasoned that we didn't know which direction was home for the poor lost pup, and we were only going north, but I quickly doubled back on that position. "I suppose we could take it with us, try to find its owner in the next town."

"Sounds like a plan," Speedo agreed, his eyes softening as he looked at the dog. "But it's joining us for the most challenging stretch of the trail. I hope it can keep up."

We packed our gear and set off into the cool morning, the anticipation of the day's trials heavy on our minds. The dog—now our unexpected companion—trotted alongside us, its wagging tail communicating its eagerness to face whatever lay ahead. I felt a camaraderie with this four-legged traveler, another soul drawn to the wild call of the trail, another member of my trail family.

"Stay close, Dog," I murmured, scratching its ears as we navigated a particularly treacherous section of rocks. "We'll get you home."

The dog seemed unfazed, its eyes glimmering as though to say, "Don't worry, I got this. It's you guys that seem to need the help."

That day, with our little canine mountaineer in tow, we reached the most difficult mile of the trail, Mahoosuc Notch. House-sized boulders dominated the view with deep crevices between, a landscape that can't really be hiked but rather slithered, clambered, and dragged through, often forcing you to remove your pack and drag it behind you through the many tight squeezes. This single mile often took some hikers upwards of three hours to complete. My trail-name was put to the test.

I glanced at "Dog," concern knitting my brow.

"Think he can handle this?" SoS responded to my look of concern.

"Think we can?" I replied.

With grim determination, we descended into the formidable notch. Every boulder demanded complete attention and creativity as we planned and executed our paths through the labyrinth. By the end, I felt like I had hiked thirty miles. My calves and forearms burned, and several new scrapes and bruises gave testament to the accomplishment. Throughout the perilous mile, Dog would disappear down a side path and reappear several times, and as I stood catching my breath past the last boulder, I heard his feet padding up to us once again.

"Good boy," I murmured. "You conquered the notch."

"That's his trail name," said SoS. "Notch."

We all agreed.

Several miles from Mahoosuc Notch, we stopped at a road crossing for a breath and to decide whether we would take the opportunity to attempt a hitch into the nearest town for food and to inquire about Notch. My muscles ached from the day's exertion, but I was filled with accomplishment at having conquered the most formidable mile on the Appalachian Trail. My companions' faces and postures reflected a similar mix of exhaustion and pride.

As I scanned the road, I noticed a man standing by his truck holding a device in his hand, turning it this way and that, looking around as if searching for something or someone. A flicker of hope ignited within me. Could this be Notch's owner?

"Excuse me," I called out hesitantly, "are you looking for a dog?"

The man turned towards us, his eyes widening as they fell upon Notch. "Mo!" he exclaimed, rushing forward to embrace the four-legged friend. "I've been looking everywhere for you, buddy!"

He looked up at us, his face full of gratitude. "Thank you so much! I can't tell you how worried I've been."

"Of course," I replied, smiling back at him. "We couldn't just leave him out there."

As Notch—or rather, Mo—wriggled and wagged his tail happily, the man introduced himself and offered to drive us into town as a token of his appreciation. We gratefully accepted, eager for a hot meal and a chance to rest our weary bodies.

During the drive, we were entertained with stories of life in Maine and this man's adventures with Mo, while SoS, Speedo, and I reciprocated with tales from the trail. It felt strangely comforting, this unexpected camaraderie forged through our shared love for the great outdoors and the companions who accompanied us along the way.

Upon reaching town, Mo's owner gave us some cash to treat ourselves to a meal. We accepted the kind offer and said our goodbyes. In a strange way, it was hard seeing the man drive off with Mo. The dog had only come into our lives that morning, but he had hiked with us, struggled with us, kept us company, and lifted our spirits. In that span of a grueling mile, Dog had become Notch, and Notch had become friend. Then, like so many others we met along the trail, he was gone, but we found comfort in knowing he was safe.

# 22

## ONE STEP AT A TIME

The day after returning Notch to his rightful owner, I woke with a new sense of clarity. As clearly as the sun rose in the sky, I rose knowing that something needed to change on this journey.

We'd spent the previous night in Bethel, where Notch's grateful owner treated us to a hearty dinner. After a satisfying breakfast, we hitched a ride back to the trail. That was a delightful experience in itself. A man and his son picked us up in their truck. When I asked where they were going, the father said, "Wherever you need us to drop you."

"You're not heading anywhere?" asked Speedo.

"Nope. I woke up this morning and told my son here, 'let's go help some hikers today.' Luckily, we came across you smelly fellers."

The kid asked us all about the trail, and we gladly shared stories, and all the time, I was distracted by just how amazing that moment was—a father showing his son the importance of going out of your way to help someone for no other reason than that they might need it.

When the man and his son dropped us off at the trail, we quickly fell back into our rhythm, hiking at a brisk pace to make up for "lost time." As soon as we took our first trail steps that day, I knew I was nearing the moment I had woken up that morning thinking about. For the last several days, it had been growing, the realization that I was no longer hiking my hike. I was hiking Speedo's hike. That was no fault of his. It was easy to fall back into that rhythm, one that felt much like the same pace of life I had lived for ten corporate years. There was a familiarity to it, a workmanlike approach, one of progress and productivity in the miles. But I was not there to produce. I was there to experience, to learn, to grow. At about mile twelve of the day, I noticed a perfect stealth camping spot nestled amongst the trees.

"Speedo," I said, panting. "I need to slow down."

He looked at me with concern. "Are you ok?"

"I'm fine," I replied, feeling a little guilty but relieved at the same time. "I just can't keep going at this pace. I need to get back to my own rhythm again. I think I'm going to stay here tonight."

I had dreaded that moment, fearing I'd hurt Speedo's feelings or cause him to be disappointed with me, two things that I shouldn't have burdened myself with in the first place. But he was fine.

"No worries, Scrambler," he said, nothing but understanding in his tone. "You gotta hike your hike, man."

We said our goodbyes. SoS decided to stick around and camp with me that night, and as I set up my tent amidst the whispering pines, I breathed deeply, feeling the weight of previous days of haste lift from my shoulders. I had returned to myself—hiking not for the destination but the journey itself.

SoS never said it in words, but I could see it in his expression that this had been a burden lifted from him as well. We were no longer bound by the expectations of another or the pressure to keep up with someone else's desire to finish. We had reclaimed our sense of adventure and re-embraced the trail on our terms.

Our camping spot sat beside a clear, trickling stream. The gentle babbling seemed to wash away the last remnants of the race I had been running, leaving a profound sense of peace in its wake.

That night, I dreamt of the endless miles I had traveled, the blisters on my feet, and the countless breathtaking sights I had seen. When I awoke the next morning, I was filled with contentment for the miles behind and excitement for the ones ahead. My thoughts turned to a quote from Paulo Coelho that had resonated with me in the year leading up to the trail: "Maybe the journey isn't so much about becoming anything. Maybe it's about un-becoming everything that isn't really you, so you can be who you were meant to be in the first place."

SoS stirred in his tent, emerging with a sleepy smile. "How are you feeling?" he asked, his voice soft and sincere.

"Great," I replied, more than just the required nicety but a real description of my current state. I could see in his eyes that he understood.

I felt a surge of gratitude. Together, we would continue onward, no longer racing against time or each other but simply embracing the beauty of the trail and the journey within ourselves.

The days that followed were a kaleidoscope of raw beauty and physical challenge. Maine's wild landscape stretched out before us as we navigated jagged peaks and craggy ridgelines offering some of the most untamed sights we had encountered on the trail.

Flowing streams crisscrossed through and along the trail, their crystal-clear waters providing soothing background music for our journey. Clear ponds accented our views, reflecting the sky above perfectly and offering a momentary respite from the challenges of the hike. Our bodies ached from the relentless terrain, but our spirits soared with each new discovery.

"Look at this," SoS said, his voice filled with wonder as we came upon a place on the edge of a lake. A small collection of canoes rested against the shoreline, an unspoken invitation for hikers to take a break and explore the tranquil waters.

"Let's do it," I agreed, excitement bubbling within me. It was a chance for us to slow down even more and truly embrace the beauty around us. We selected a sturdy-looking canoe and carefully pushed off, our paddles slicing through the tranquil water of the serene lake. I don't know how much time we spent gliding along the reflective surface, it didn't matter. We weren't measuring our journey in minutes or hours or days, but experiences.

Another experience found us beside a particularly restful stream, its gentle babbles coaxing us to stop and simply listen. As we sat on sun-warmed rocks, I challenged myself to think only on how much I had come to appreciate clean, flowing water during my time on the trail—a meditation. It was a simple pleasure, yet one that held immeasurable value.

Another day, SoS and I came to another road crossing and found ourselves hitching into a nearby town for supplies. Standing on the edge of the road, we stuck out our thumbs and hoped for a kindhearted stranger to stop and give us a ride. The minutes ticked by slowly, but I didn't feel the usual impatience or anxiety that might have plagued us before. In weeks prior, this half-hour wait might have seemed like a waste of precious time. But now, standing there in the warm sunlight, the wind rustling the trees overhead, I saw how every moment could be just as valuable as any other if I allowed myself to be fully there in it.

As we waited, I took in the sights around us: shades of green swaying gently with quivering leaves, the occasional bird flitting from branch to branch, offering brief notes of song, the faint scents of the wilderness carried on the breeze. All these sensory details were no longer distractions from discomfort felt in my muscles and bones, but gifts that enriched my heart and soul.

Saddleback Mountain rose up out of the forest in front of us, a long, high ridge described by trail guides as a particularly challenging stretch. My body still ached as much as it ever had, but as we began our ascent, I was invigorated. Saddleback stretched for miles, accented by large rocks strewn about like a giant had taken a hoe and tilled up this lofty stretch of earth. But unhurried, I felt less taxed than I had during previous legs of the Whites and even during far flatter and easier terrain. I stopped at several locations to pause and take in a view from a tall boulder or spring trickling down the side of the ridge. Saddleback Mountain would not be remembered for its difficulty, not even when the rain came down and turned the paths between tall rocks into free-flowing streams. It would be remembered for the moments.

The next day, we celebrated the 2,000-mile mark of the trail. As we arrived at the milestone, I stopped and shook my head at how crazy it seemed to have walked that far. SoS paused beside me.

"Two thousand miles…" he said.

I nodded silently.

I felt a strong desire to do something grand to celebrate the monumental moment, but could think of nothing that seemed enough. I settled for staying put awhile. SoS and I made a "2000" out of fallen branches, and I hoped the hikers after us would see it and find some meaning and encouragement.

"Well done, SoS," I said.

"You too, Scrambler."

That night, as we gathered around a campfire, and the weight of the day's hike settled into my muscles, I pulled out my phone to check for any messages from friends and family, as I had done each night. Most of the time, I didn't have enough signal, and that was just fine, preferred actually; I wanted to be careful with my distractions. That night, I had just enough connection to receive some unwanted news.

"Did you know Keep Up?" I asked SoS quietly.

"No," he replied.

"I hiked a lot with him in the middle states. He got injured…had to end his hike early, not far behind us."

The news hit me like a punch in the gut, and even though SoS hadn't met Keep Up, I could see that it affected him too. To think that he had come all that way, to leave the trail so close to the end...

We sat in silence, the magnitude of Keep Up's departure settling over us like a shroud. As the fire burned low, my thoughts turned inward, considering the state of my own body. I was breaking down, the relentless miles taking their toll on me with each passing day.

"Slowing down was the right choice," I said, staring into the dying embers. I remembered once again just how close I had come to ending my hike early and imagined just how excruciating that would have felt, knowing I was rushing the miles at the time. Then it hit me...

"Not because it is safer," I added. "This isn't really ever safe. What happened to Keep Up could happen to any of us, no matter how careful we are. This journey isn't about finishing—it's about being here, truly living. I'd rather hike only a mile and really experience it than the whole trail, just trying to be done, you know?"

SoS nodded, "One step at a time."

As the fire burned out that night, my heart ached for Keep Up, but I was filled with gratitude.

I'd keep that promise to myself, one step at a time.

# 23

**A PROMISE AND A FRIEND**

"You guys are all starting to look the same. You all have these beards, and you're in such great health!"

She wasn't wrong, the elderly lady who said this to me as I was putting in my first twenty-miler in Maine. By this point, any male thru-hiker—unless they have a massive aversion to facial hair and are willing to cope with the weight of unnecessary supplies—is likely to have a full Zach Brown Band look on their face. They were also likely to be about as physically streamlined a version of themselves as possible from the extreme calorie spend. Earlier in the hike, the woman's comment might have been more of a question: "Where are you heading?" or "Are you hiking the entire trail?" Now, our physical appearances seemed to nullify that line of questioning.

Regarding the accuracy of her observations, I held a mixture of feelings for it. There was the obvious contrast of being compared to the "normal" person, the non-thru-hiker. Counter-intuitively, those feelings had mostly diminished the further the trail wore on and the more "different" I appeared. On the other hand, the fact that my appearance elicited such an irresistible response from this woman also made the rapid approach of the end more real. The bushier my beard, the closer I was to Katahdin. It was coming soon, ready or not. I wasn't sure which I was.

The days melted into a blur of introspection while I did my best to attend to what was going on around me and avoid the thoughts of what came next. It was a constant battle.

Some moments served to pull my thoughts away from Katahdin, such as the crossing of the Kennebec River, the first and only time I had to ferry on the AT. The sign "Kennebec River Ferry Service" conjured images in my head of ferrying over the Hudson from my time working in NYC, but this was anything but. A man ushered you into a small canoe like any other you might rent at a campground except for one subtle but important difference—a single white blaze painted on the bottom indicating that this was, in fact, the Appalachian Trail.

Of course, blueberries stand out in my memory from the remaining miles. That sweet, fresh taste was always and immediately a reset for my mind.

The vistas continued to amaze, the trail still serene and enchanting, but no matter how many observations I found, my thoughts always returned to Katahdin. *What will it feel like cresting the final peak? Where will this journey leave me when it's over? What comes next?* My mood was somber, contemplative, a stark contrast to the excitement and wonder I'd felt so often throughout my time out there. It wasn't so much Katahdin that constantly pulled on my thoughts but the "what's after?" of Katahdin. I had felt so connected to the people and places of the trail and to the trail itself. I couldn't stop wondering whether that would continue after the end of it.

After I shaved and raised my body fat back into the normal range, would I still feel like the outsider to so many who had not gone through this experience?

The morning I crossed the Kennebec, there was a crisp teasing of autumn in the air, but not yet any sign of it in the full summer coloring on the leaves. We were treated to a delicious breakfast at the Caratunk Bed and Breakfast on the other side, and I tried to savor each bite of my eggs and toast, committing the flavors to memory. Ordinary things tasted so different on the trail, flavors became fuller and more alive. Would I remember that? Or would I forget the strange elation that accompanied things I had for so long considered normal and abundant?

There were times during those miles when I was so much in my head that I often went miles before remembering I wasn't alone. SoS was still with me and Lieutenant Dan had rejoined us at a point I couldn't remember. Other times, those moments would have been made more vivid and warm because of the camaraderie. The night after crossing the Kennebec, we camped next to a pond so still and glassy, we were treated to the light of two moons. Despite the calming beauty of the scene, I was unable to sleep, my thoughts inevitably drifting toward Katahdin. It seemed no amount of focus could hold me to the present moment, a thing I had worked so hard to foster.

The next day, I stumbled into the Appalachian Trail Conservancy in Monson, Maine, and I was lifted from my stupor long enough to put pen to paper and register to summit Katahdin on September 5th. With trembling hands, I signed my name on the ledger, my heart pounding in my chest. I cried for the millionth time. This time, my tears were accompanied by an uneasy mixture of elation and dread. The end was so close, and I couldn't shake the feeling that I might just not be ready for it.

"Are you okay?" Lieutenant Dan asked, his brow furrowed in concern.

I nodded but couldn't find the words to express the storm of emotions brewing within me. Instead, I excused myself and stepped outside, pulling out my phone to call my mom.

"Hi!" she answered, her voice strong and excited. "How are you doing?"

My throat tightened, and I struggled to speak. Even if I could have mustered the power to speak through the choke in my throat, I don't think I would have known just what to say. I was fine. I was a wreck. I was ready to be done. I wanted to stay out there forever. All of these were true, and yet, none of those encapsulated how I felt. Not truly. Not fully.

"Mom…" I finally whispered, my voice cracking with emotion. "I'm almost there…I'm just not sure where that is."

Her response was immediate and fierce. "You just climb that mountain, Ryan. You'll figure out what next means when it comes."

Each time I'd received support from my family, it had been a source of strength, a fuel for this difficult journey. But now, I didn't need the will to continue. I knew I would make it. I didn't know exactly what I needed.

Entering the 100-mile wilderness provided a little relief. I had stepped back into a world of dense forests and rugged terrain that felt familiar, a complete isolation and remoteness that had become like a friend returned to be with me for the last of the journey. It was as though Maine had no need for civilization and had kept it away, leaving only the raw, untamed beauty of the wilderness for those needing to return to it. It was almost jarring in the best way I could imagine, and for a time, I was transported from the anxious thoughts and returned to the beauty around me.

But as we ventured deeper into the wilderness, I began to remember that even this place had a beginning and therefore an end. Soon enough, I would find it.

"Scrambler, you okay?" SoS asked at one point.

"Yeah," I said, not sure it was the entire truth. "Just taking it all in."

It was day 121 when my sixth pair of trail shoes carried me to the 2,100-mile mark. I had already glued them from heel to toe, trying to coax them through the final miles. But I wasn't thinking about whether my shoes would hold up. I was only aware of the last century mark I got to celebrate before my hike was over. I stopped in my tracks, staring at the dirt beneath me as if it held some hidden meaning, some secret message that would help me understand the whirlwind of emotions coursing through me. I had cried most days on the trail, and as I stood there at the twenty-first and last hundred-mile crossing, I added to this tradition; only this time, I felt something like numbness, or maybe an avoidance of feeling as the tears welled up. I felt like I had just lost something precious and was about to lose more.

Lieutenant Dan, SoS, and I shared a solemn nod, and in silence, we continued along the narrow path.

The next four days were much of the same—gazing into the distance or at the nearby thick vegetation or down at my feet finding their way along the path, all the while seeing mere glimpses of the environment around me outside of what filled the vision of my mind—the constant mirage of a life unknown, beyond the life that had come to feel so familiar and natural and real. At the end of those four days, we left the 100-mile Wilderness and crossed the Abol bridge over the West Branch Penobscot River.

At the end of the bridge, we stumbled into the small restaurant. I eagerly stepped inside, suddenly ravenous for a hot meal. I had kept correspondence up with my coordinates with other thru-hikers as a safety precaution in case I went missing. Little did I know, one of those I coordinated with was using that information for a particular purpose. As I sat in the restaurant watching the rain gently tap against the window, I heard a familiar voice.

"Hey, Scrambler."

I turned, and there was BAMF standing beside me. My eyes filled with tears as I stood, unable to contain the overwhelming wave of emotion that swept through me.

"Wh-what are you doing here?" I managed to choke out.

"Did you really think I'd let you finish this journey alone?" BAMF grinned. He had driven over eight hours from his home in Montreal, Canada, to live up to his promise to hike Katahdin with me.

We embraced like proud men rarely do, and my tears flowed freely down my cheeks.

"Thank you," I said.

"Of course..." he replied, "of course."

The next day, BAMF and I hiked into Baxter State Park, where we would spend the final night at the base of Katahdin. During the miles that day, we came upon a waterfall.

"This is what I miss the most," said BAMF.

"Same," I said, "Just being surrounded by natural beauty, day in and day out."

Then it dawned on me. To be immersed in nature doesn't require hiking the Appalachian Trail. It's all around. I only needed to choose to put myself there.

# 24

## A NEW FIRST DAY

I had a week's worth of dirt caked onto my calves. I was physically, mentally, and emotionally tired. I was exhausted like I had never been before in my life—exhausted from the 126 days before, maybe even more exhausted thinking about the one day left. This was the last day, the one in which I would do the last thing I was here to do—summit Mt. Katahdin, finish thru-hiking the Appalachian Trail, then meet what was on the other side.

Tired as I was, I couldn't sleep. I didn't sleep, not one minute. I thought about every inch of every mile of every day. I scanned through the difficulties and the triumphs, each inextricably linked to the other. I saw the faces I'd met, the towns I'd visited, the waterfalls with all their powerful grace, and the peaks and valleys, the ones I saw and the ones I felt. I saw everything like it was a movie playing in my mind, and I did this all night long. I didn't even try to shut it off. I knew I couldn't, and I decided I didn't want to. I was afraid to fall asleep, afraid that if I did, I would miss something, some last moment I would want to keep with me always.

When the sun began to brighten the sky, I watched it happen. Already, my sight was blurred with the tears for every inch of every mile, for the last 126 days, and for the last one I had before me. I stood, and as I rolled up my sleeping pad, stretched, and packed my bag for the last time, those tears brimmed and streamed down my salty, dirty face. I had cried nearly every day on the trail. This day, I would cry nearly every step.

As promised 126 days before, and fulfilled by his surprise reappearance, BAMF was with me, and he was not without emotion either. It was the first time neither of us said anything to the other at breakfast or during the morning hike. We didn't have to say anything because we understood exactly what the other was feeling, at least as well as we could understand it within ourselves.

When we left basecamp that morning and took our first steps up the ascent, the weather was as predicted—hazy, cold, breezy, not what you would have drawn up if the weather was yours to command. There was no grand view of the last great peak. There didn't need to be. The fog was exactly what it needed to be, a reminder of so many moments on the trail that had the power to teach me what I needed, not what I had come to get—that you could not turn off the rain on the trail just like you couldn't in life, that you cannot always have what you desire, but you can always want what you already have, that wishing for a different reality was the thief of joy in the current.

The fog forced my gaze inward, and I did my best to quiet my mind, to take the steps and to see and feel myself taking them, the crunch of rocks and dirt beneath my feet, the rising slope, the cool air clinging to my legs. I breathed slowly and looked upon the available scenery without praise or judgement of what I was seeing, and without praise or judgement of myself. I didn't think. I just felt. And what I felt amazed me—calmness, satiation, the peace that comes from not wanting, not hoping, and not worrying about the next moment or the previous. I felt complete. I hadn't even reached the steep part of the ascent, but I felt as if I had already summited and come back down.

I smiled, fresh tears clinging to the rim of my eyes as I walked, and time seemed to disappear. It might have been hours or minutes passing, and I don't know if I could have told the difference.

Then I saw it, the top of my trail, the peak of my journey, and the iconic sign that stands there to this day, a small a-frame sign, not made of wood as it appears but of the cumulative dreams of so many. I began to sob. I felt whole, happy, and ready.

I reached the sign, and I had no thoughts, only feeling, only instinct. And still, I heaved and sobbed, inhaled and sobbed. I gave the sign a big kiss and rested my forehead on it. Then a surge, an unignorable desire fueled by everything that came before, overtook me. I have never felt like that before or since, and the closest I can come to describing it is an unignorable, happy rage. Like an animal uncaged, I climbed the sign. I stood as high into the air as it would let me, and that wasn't high enough. So, I stretched my arms into the air until I felt the joints of my shoulders might pop, trekking poles clutched in my hands.

And then I roared.

Like the free, uncaged beast I was, I roared with not one feeling but the cumulated emotions of every step of every day before and during the trail. I roared from the power of a thousand should-ons released—the shame, the guilt, the failure, and all the life I knew I had left to live—all of it erupted from my lungs like a geyser from the molten earth.

I didn't stay long at Katahdin's summit. I hadn't come to linger. I hadn't stepped onto the trail to linger either. I had come for the journey, for a new way to know myself and the world around me. I took pictures of some other hikers. Others took some of me. Then I left and began the descent back down the slope.

The tears were gone, replaced. The fear I had felt for that moment at various times throughout the journey, for coming to the end, for wondering what would come next—that was replaced as well with a contentment, a trusting in myself and in the world. I knew I was ready to be off the trail because the journey hadn't really ended. I had simply learned a new way to live, both on the trail and off the trail. Whatever came next, I would live that way.

I would choose to be present, to take in every single moment as if it were my very last, to enjoy this life with the people I love the most. I would help when I could. I would accept help when offered. I would connect authentically with others. I would love fiercely. I would be kind, remembering how just one simple act could change someone's journey in a positive way.

More than all of this, I would share these experiences whenever, however I could, with everyone. The trail had ended, but the journey continued. I had chosen myself, and in doing so, I had chosen everyone. In hiking the Appalachian Trail, I learned the most valuable lesson of my life, that in order to be happy, I never needed to hike the Appalachian Trail. I didn't need to swim the English Channel or climb Mt. Everest. Dreams don't have to be big; they just have to be my own.

I could have done any or all of those things and not been happy doing them. Many have and aren't. To be happy, happy in the way that doesn't come one moment and leave the next, I simply had to choose it. To be present, connected, and true to myself, those would be the white blazes marking the trail. I only needed to move in the direction of my heart. If I did that, come rain or sun, I'd be able to smile with them both.

I stopped on the downward slopes of Katahdin and looked back a moment, just briefly, and I saw not the top of a mountain, nor the last day of a long journey, but the first day of the rest of my life.

# EPILOGUE

## STILL WANDERING

"Dad, I did it."

He was the first call I made after descending from the peak of Katahdin.

"I'm so, so proud of you," he replied.

I couldn't remember him saying those words at any time prior in my life. I knew he was always proud of me, but there was something different about this moment. It wasn't completing the AT that made him proud. It was that I had been completely lost but found the courage to change my life. I had opened up, sought help, and put myself on a new path.

If you've made it this far in my story, what I'm about to say will come as no shock. Coming to the end of the trail and having left so much of my previous life behind, what weighed heaviest on my mind was the question of what's next? How could I be a "trail angel" off the trail? A few things I knew for certain:

1) I wanted to share everything I went through with those I felt could benefit from it most—the adventure, the hardships, the lessons learned, the internal, the external—all of it. So

many times, after I had completed the hike, I wished I'd known before starting the journey just how much that experience would benefit me. I wished someone in my life had pulled me aside and said to me, "Hey Ryan, have you considered another path?" I could be that person for someone else, and I would be.

2) I would never trap myself in an office again. And it would have been so easy to do, to default back to what was familiar and financially secure. But I simply don't believe human beings thrive when spending most of their waking hours sitting in a fluorescent box. The value of regular daylight access to nature is too great. Scientists are constantly learning more ways it improves our physical and mental health. And there is nothing more fundamentally important to our overall happiness and fulfillment in life than our own personal health. Thoreau might have said it best when he recalled, "I went to the woods and came out taller than the trees."

3) And most important of all, whatever I did, it would always be authentically and entirely me, and I was okay with that being a moving target—a person should always be allowed to grow.

With these three criteria in mind, I set about figuring out what all that meant for my future. I visited a friend in California, and he asked a question I was not surprised by: "How does it feel to start all over?" Meaning financially. I was surprised when I responded, "I feel richer than ever before," and meant it. It was the first time I realized I was beginning to measure wealth apart from money.

I had spent ten years making money doing soul-crushing work but never having "enough." But just because I was choosing to live a life centered around freedom of time and place, that did not mean I was immune to the fact that living required food and shelter, and in the world we live in, that means at least some amount of consistent income. How could I take the experiences I had gained and the goals for my future life and marry them in a way that provided for that life?

I had spent a good amount of time reading and practicing mindfulness in the months leading up to, during, and after the trail, and I was confident I was on the right path. I knew without seeing them yet that opportunities would open up to me. All I had to do was stay true to who I was becoming and keep becoming him.

I supposed that, more than anything else, was what I wanted to share—the ability to stop and calmly reflect on oneself, to be intentional about making our own choices, rather than being herded into our "decisions" by others. In thinking about this, I realized that if I hoped to offer any of this to anyone, I needed to decide who I was offering it to. That was an easy one, young people. That was when I knew I could have used this perspective the most, those years when I was actively making decisions about what my life was going to be…the first time. School-age kids, college students, young adults just entering the workforce, even career persons like I had been, wondering if the life path they have set out on is the right one for them—these were the people I could help the most.

Perfect, I had an audience! But where would I engage these people, and how would I get them to agree to be there in the first place? This was the difficult part. I had radically changed my life, done something that most would agree is difficult in an extreme way, and learned so much that could benefit so many. But I couldn't just start cold-calling parents asking to chat with their kids. "Umm… Mrs. Jones, I was wondering if I could speak with your son about his future. And would you mind paying me?"

As I pondered this, I realized the only way I could reach a gathering of people in one place was to go to the place those people were already gathering. If I wanted to share my story with middle-school students, for instance, I would need to visit a middle school.

That was the lightbulb moment. I won't bore you with pages of details of how I went from there to where I am now. You didn't pick up this book to learn how to grow a business, and that's not what this story is about. But I do want to tell you where I am because *that* is what this book is about—not me, specifically, but about how choosing your own path and making it…truly…*your own* path is never the wrong decision. I want you to give yourself permission to really believe that, so I want to give you the hope and example necessary to believe that it is true.

Since I left Katahdin, exactly six years ago as of September 5th, 2023, the day of the publication of this book, I've been fortunate to share my story at numerous grade schools, colleges, corporations, associations, communities, and societies. I've led countless group wilderness therapies, motivational workshops, and coached many groups and individuals about life and opportunities and how to think about those things in ways that aren't always apparent. These opportunities have taken me all around the globe and given me more experiences that have allowed me to continue growing and to continue wandering. I'm happy to report that I've been able to pay all of my bills doing this.

Perhaps more important than any of this, the book, or any of the work I've done over these last six years is the fact that I've found love again. I've started a family, becoming a father and soon-to-be husband to my son's mother, the love of my life. And I can proudly say that for my son's first two years, I've spent more time looking straight into his eyes than at a television or phone screen.

We have built a home together, not just a house filled with things, and we have a life where presence with each other is our priority. The return on that investment has been greater than any I could think of. Before, I had convinced myself I didn't want kids. The truth was, I didn't know how to love and be present with myself, much less do it for another. Now, my greatest priority has become being a loving and present partner and father. That is the greatest gift I can give, not just to them, but myself.

I thought I was just slowing down. Instead, I was beginning to live. I hope you will too.

Never stop wandering.

If you'd like to know more about the ways I engage and share value, please visit my webpage at:

RyanBenz.com

Or drop me a line at:
Ryan@RyanBenz.com

# ACKNOWLEDGEMENTS

I once believed I had to figure all this out on my own, but this journey would not have been possible without the love and support of so many.

To my partner, Maghee, for loving and supporting me beyond measure. Thank you for not just listening to me talk about this book for the last six years but motivating me to keep going and to share it with the world. I wake up every single day feeling grateful to walk this path with you, that our collective steps led me to you, and you to me in the first place. You've always wondered if anything would ever top the AT in my mind. Well, it's been topped. It's you and our family that have been my greatest journey of all. You never let me forget that life and love matter most. And finally, thank you for the prompt, "What made you happy today?" That kept me going.

And to our son, Remy. You have completely changed the way I see the world, my place in it, and my true purpose, forever.

Special thanks to:

Mom and Dad, for believing in me and supporting me every step of the way. Through that, you've shown me the greatest gift I can ever provide to my own children.

My brother, for being there when I needed it most. That simple act of encouraging me to explore a new way of being in the world; that changed my life forever, and I hope you know that.

My sister, for the continuous love and support and for showing me what it means to follow your dreams.

My team. To Shawn, my writing consultant, for believing in this story and helping me find my voice so I could put it all down on paper. To my editor, Jessi, for pushing this book to be what it is. To my designer, Mirko, for laying out the words on these pages and for all the inspiration. To Kerry, for working with me to include the amazing hand-drawn map. And thank you to my good friend and creative genius, Luke. Most importantly, for supporting me throughout this entire journey and also for designing the cover of this book. This truly required a team, and it has been an honor working alongside all of you.

To my niece and nephews, thank you for reminding me to never lose my childlike wonder.

Thank you to all the people who encouraged me over the last six years since stepping off the trail to write this book. The occasional, "How's that book coming along?" was a constant guidance and more helpful than you know.

To all my friends and family who came out of their way during my journey to be a trail angel, whether in person or online. There are far too many of you to list you all; just know that it was your encouragement that kept me going.

For all the other hikers I shared the trail with that year— thru-hikers, section hikers, day hikers, even if just for the briefest of moments—thank you for being a part of my journey. Whether we hiked a stretch together, enjoyed a meal, or shared a simple hello, smile, or fist bump, it wouldn't have been the same without you.

And to those who continue to support me today, let's keep wandering... together.

Made in the USA
Las Vegas, NV
09 December 2024

13717952R00132